MAIL-ORDER
MYSTERIES

MAIL-ORDER MYSTERIES

Real Stuff from Old Comic Book Ads!

Name by KIRK DEMARAIS

Address .... **Zip** ....

Afterword by JESSE THORN

INSIGHT EDITIONS

San Rafael, California

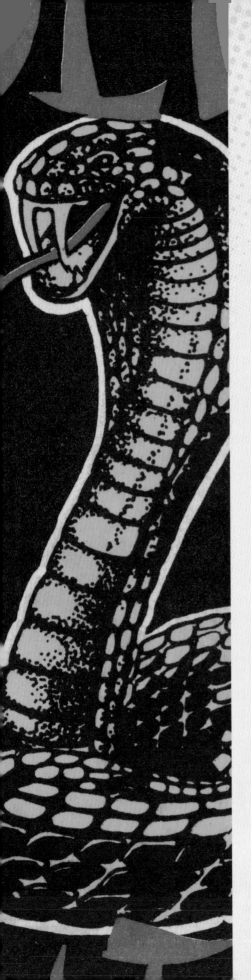

FOR DAD

INSIGHT EDITIONS

P.O. BOX 3088
San Rafael, CA 94912
www.insighteditions.com

Library of Congress Cataloging-in-Publication Data available.

ISBN: 978-1-60887-026-4

Manufactured in China by Insight Editions

10 9 8 7 6 5 4 3 2 1

 REPLANTED PAPER

 Insight Editions, in association with Roots of Peace, will
plant two trees for each tree used in the manufacturing of
ROOTS of PEACE this book. Roots of Peace is an internationally renowned
humanitarian organization dedicated to eradicating land
mines worldwide and converting war-torn lands into productive farms
and wildlife habitats. Together, we will plant two million fruit and nut
trees in Afghanistan and provide farmers there with the skills and support
necessary for sustainable land use.

CONTENTS

INTRODUCTION

I WAS A FIRST-GRADER on a routine visit to the neighborhood gas mart when I was first confronted by the newly installed tower rack of comic books. In an instant I was at the mercy of the colorful spinning column overflowing with eye-punching artwork, tantalizing characters, and glimpses into unseen worlds.

I had no choice but to forfeit my candy money for a copy of *Micronauts #9*.

As I camped out on my bedroom carpet thumbing through the baffling story line, I found myself on the verge of buyer's remorse. I should have just played it safe with my usual Fun Dip and Lik-A-Stix. Then I turned to an overcrowded page of fascinating black-and-white drawings; I was captivated. It was an ink-smudged window into an unfamiliar realm where gorilla masks peacefully lived among hovercrafts and ventriloquist dummies. It was the latest ad from the Johnson Smith Company, a novelty distributor that had been honing their catalog since 1914. A dozen pages later an outfit called the Fun Factory featured another full-page assortment of wonders, and elsewhere in the issue I found a hundred toy soldiers for a buck, an offer for a free million dollar bank note, and an ad for something called *Grit*.

To me the ads' seductive nature was the result of a powerful combination of factors. Most obviously, the products were otherworldly: X-ray vision, karate courses, a money-counterfeiting device—they almost seemed too good to be true. For the first time I wasn't thinking in terms of playthings; these were life-enhancers that offered the means to satisfy a familiar range of wish-fulfillment, including power, glory, revenge, and romance. The assortment was also more "grown-up" than the stuff in my toy box. Much of it was designed to deceive, horrify, and even humiliate; the selection was exotic, like nothing I had access to at the local toy aisle. The mysterious listings, with their vague line art and impossible descriptions, were far more intriguing than the tell-all photos of the *Sears Wishbook*. They teased my mind, causing me to ponder each item long after the book was shut. They left questions that I gleefully answered with fantasy and youthful optimism.

Due to a parental policy, the mystery remained unsolved throughout my youth. "It's a rip-off" was the motto that stood between me and the solutions to all of my problems, which included bullies, bad skin, and the inability to see through clothing. In an effort to quench my desires, my father tried to debunk each listing. Dad's arguments made sense at the time, and I agreed that I'd rather invest in something I trusted, like a new *Star Wars* figure. But what if dad was wrong? It's not like he followed every scientific advancement; maybe someone had just made a new breakthrough in ventriloquism.

As the years passed my mind never stopped trying to decipher those enigmatic listings. The unresolved puzzles stayed stranded in my childhood, and my preoccupation didn't fade with time—it intensified.

Then came the Internet, and more importantly, eBay, which presented an unexpected second chance for me to acquire these mail-order miracles and quench my curiosity at long last. Through years of online auctions I've tracked down many of the lost treasures of my childhood, often spending twenty to fifty times their original listed value. It's a small price to pay to uncover life's greatest secrets. It's also worth it to experience the joy of anticipation as, finally, my own pair of X-Ray Spex lumbered through the postal system. Of course, these days if a seller takes four to six weeks for delivery, at least I can leave negative feedback.

The author in fourth grade, proudly displaying his treasures.

As my collection started taking shape, I soon realized that Dad was right. Nearly everything is smaller, flimsier, simpler, or more inflatable than I imagined it to be. As a kid I would have been devastated, but now the objects are symbols of a bigger story. As a consensual participant in the long-standing tradition of mail-order letdowns, I welcome the role of the rube and revel in the lackluster surprises that fill my mailbox.

The Internet has also united me with the legions of childhood comic buyers: both the high-functioning individuals who actually ordered the stuff and the ones like myself who never overcame the obstacles, be they parents, finances, or even living in a country unserviced by the dealers. While the enthusiasm surrounding these ads has made the leap into the digital age, there is a growing void of sound information and photographic evidence of these arcane items. This book, which documents my findings thus far, is my contribution to the cause.

The curiosities in this volume are mostly from the late 1960s and 1970s, when the market had reached a summit and every comic book doubled as a printed novelty shop. For me the collection represents so many things: a series of hard-earned revelations, my remaining sense of wonder, and the coming-of-age discovery that even kids need to be shrewd as serpents lest they get bit by one.

For others I hope that it might serve to scratch a lifelong itch or provide a journey to a magical time, or perhaps even stand as a missing chapter in the history of comic book collecting.

—Kirk Demarais

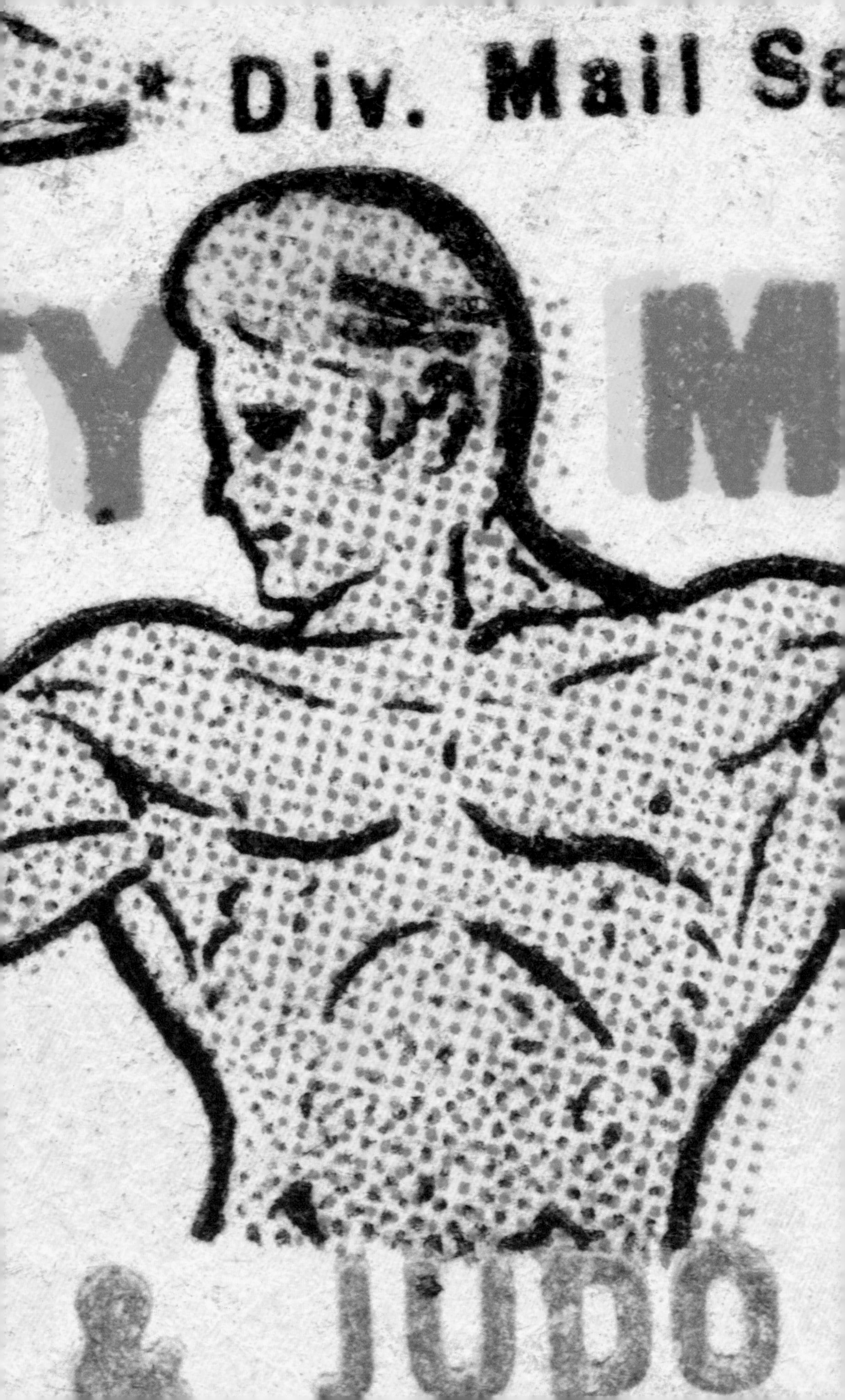
* Div. Mail Sa
Y
M
& JUDO

SUPERPOWERS AND SPECIAL ABILITIES

Ever since that guy from Krypton showed up, superhero titles have dominated the comic book scene. The stories created a yearning for superhuman abilities, and the novelty dealers were standing by to sell them. Suddenly, super strength, X-ray vision, martial arts skills, and even mind control were all within reach. For those looking for something more subtle than superhero status, the ads offered the means to become a ventriloquist, an instant guitarist, or a reporter for Archie comics. A new you was just a postage stamp away.

X-Ray Spex

- See bones thru skin
- See thru clothing...

$2.95

AMAZING X·RAY VISION Guaranteed!

#117

X-RAY VISION

THE FAMOUS *Blushingly* FUNNY ILLUSION

X-RAY SPEX

AMAZING X-RAY VISION INSTANTLY!

A HILARIOUS LAUGHINGLY FUNNY ILLUSION!

See through **fingers** - through skin - see yolk of egg - - see lead in pencil. Many, many, amazing, astounding, Illusory X-Ray views yours to see ALWAYS- -when YOU wear Slimline X-Ray Specs. Bring them to parties, for real FUN - - GUARANTEED - - They give you a 3 dimensional X-Ray Vision - - the Instant you put them on. When you look at your friends you'll "see" the most (blushingly funny) amazing things! Full Instructions Of How To Enjoy Them To The Fullest! Last For Years - - Harmless - - Requires No Electricity - - Or Batteries - - Comes Complete - - Permanently Focused - - Nothing Else to Buy - - Send $1. plus 25¢ for postage and handling - - Money Back If Not 100% Satisfied.

SLIMLINE COMPANY
Dept. 248   P.O. Box 90
285 Market Street   Newark, New Jersey

$1.

Surprise your friends with X-RAY sight!

MAIL COUPON TODAY!

SLIMLINE COMPANY, Dept. **248**
285 Market Street, Newark, New Jersey

I enclose $1 plus 25¢ for postage and handling (Total ($1.25) send me the Slimline X-RAY SPECS. My money will be refunded in full if I am not 100% Satisfied.
Send me. . . . . sets at $1.25 per set.
Total enclosed is $. . . . .
My money will be refunded in full if I am not 100% Satisfied.
Name . . . .
Address . . . .
City & State . . . . .

WE IMAGINED: Glasses that enable you to see real skeletons and nudity.

THEY SENT: Eyewear stuffed with bird feathers. Really! In the original Spex the X-ray illusion occurs as the viewer looks through genuine feathers, which are embedded between the cardboard layers of the lenses. The feather's vanes diffract light, creating the appearance of two offset images. A darker area forms where the images overlap, which can be interpreted as the bones in your hand or the curves of a lady.

BEHIND THE MYSTERY: X-Ray Spex came about in 1964 when Harold von Braunhut (the mastermind behind Sea-Monkeys) repackaged an optical effect made popular by a device called the Wonder Tube. The Spex were so successful, they spawned various iterations (see page 12).

CUSTOMER SATISFACTION:
Not X-actly what we X-pected, but they're X-alted as the quintessential mail-order novelty.

ABOVE: Eventually the manufacturers discontinued the use of plastic frames and began producing X-Ray Spex entirely out of cardstock. To the right is the view through a pair of X-Ray Spex.

AQUA-SPEX

Harold von Braunhut's seeing aids also included Aqua-Spex, which were said to enable underwater viewing for fishermen. The frames are identical to their brethren, but these lenses sport tiny plastic levers that rotate the tinted plastic within. This enables the wearer to adjust the degree of tinting according to how much surface glare is present. Once you find the ideal setting, the water is said to "vanish like magic."

See Underwater

Aqua-Vision glasses. Fantastic aid that enables you to see right into the water. New optical principle eliminates surface glare. Makes looking into the water like seeing into an aquarium. Great fishing aid, as well as for nature study.
☐ **9252. Price Postpaid** **$1.25**

"Catch-a-Pet" AQUA-SPEX

AT LAST! A WAY TO SEE UNDER WATER FROM ABOVE THE SURFACE

Spot and capture Turtles, Frogs and other creatures hidden in ponds, streams, etc..

BRING HOME MORE LIVE PETS FROM THE COUNTRY OR SEASHORE

HYPNO-SPEX

Rounding out Harold von Braunhut's trifecta of superpowered eyewear are the Amazing Dunninger's Hypno-Spex. The familiar frames are filled this time with the same lenticular spiral design that is used in the classic Hypno-Coin. The instructions provide steps for inducing sleep by tilting the glasses up and down so that the spirals appear to spin. As a bonus, there's a section on how to humiliate naysayers by causing them to lose their balance onstage.

DUNNINGER'S HYPNO-SPEX

Hypno-Spex created by Dunninger, the greatest mastermind of them all! Incredible results with electrifying speed. Millions saw these hypnotic glasses work on Johnny Carson's national TV show. Professional results guaranteed.
☐ **3764. Hypno-Spex** **$1.49**

HYPNO-COIN

HYPNO-COIN. Free with 25 LESSONS IN HYPNOTISM. Do you realize the power that hypnotism will give you? With the magic power of hypnosis you can hypnotize at a glance, make people obey your commands, strengthen your memory, develop a strong personality, overcome bad habits. 25 lessons covers this and much more. Order now and receive new patented HYPNO-COIN Free.

☐ No. 130 $1.00

WE IMAGINED: The ability to control other human beings, girls in particular.

THEY SENT: A pamphlet first produced in the 1920s and a plastic disc with a lenticular surface that makes the spiral design rotate. The instructions outline techniques that have been seen in old movies and TV shows for decades. However, they prove to be less successful when applied to people who aren't paid actors.

CUSTOMER SATISFACTION: Overpowering disappointment.

MAKE YOUR PATIENT COMFORTABLE ON A SOFA. TELL HER TO RELAX HER MUSCLES, AND SEE THAT SHE DOES

25 Lessons HYPNOTISM

VENTRILOQUIST DUMMY

Have Fun & Entertain

Bargain Price $2.95

Ventriloquist Dummies

Full length 16-inch dummies with control to operate mouth & move head. Learn to throw your voice & entertain friends. Make them sit, stand, even dance & act alive! Fully dressed in colorful clothing. Moulded plastic. Natural finish. Movable arms & legs.

☐ 6156. Archy The Dummy $2.95
☐ 6075. Dumbo The Clown $2.95

WE IMAGINED: Our ticket to stardom.

THEY SENT: Hollow figures that are no more than plastic heads, hands, and boots held together with scrap fabric, cardboard, and rubber bands. Archy (spelled "Archie" in later ads) and Dumbo are less than half the size of the typical ventriloquial figures found in toy shops. In the rare event that the mouth mechanics work, the string functions opposite to that of a "real" dummy, and the "natural finish" claim is grossly inaccurate.

CUSTOMER SATISFACTION: Hollow and lifeless.

BELOW: Archy's innards and Archy compared to a standard-size figure.

VENTRILO VOICE THROWER

THROW YOUR VOICE

Throw your voice into trunks, behind doors, everywhere. Instrument fits in your mouth and out of sight. Fool teacher, friends and family. Free book on "How to Become a Ventriloquist." No. 137 25¢

VENTRILO
THE WONDER VOICE THROWER
Directions: Dip the Ventrillo in water, then place between lips and blow through either opening until sound comes through. Then place on tongue and press it against roof of mouth and hiss strongly through it, until sound is clear. Then practice talking and other imitations.

WE IMAGINED: A secret instrument that enables you to project your voice to any location or from inside any object in the room.

THEY SENT: Two half-inch metal pieces bound by a pink ribbon. As your breath passes between the metal slats, they vibrate together. This generates an otherworldly sound akin to a tiny man in a can. If you're skilled enough to operate it from the roof of your mouth (rather than your lips), you can speak words while you use it. It could pass for a "Help, let me out of here!" kind of voice if it weren't so plainly coming from your own face. While the sound effect is pretty neat, the "voice thrower" promise is bunk.

CUSTOMER SATISFACTION: Their claims are hard to swallow, but the Ventrilo isn't.

BIRD CALL

WE IMAGINED: A small, easy-to-use bird call.

THEY SENT: The Candy-Bird, or Swiss Warbler, is a leather flap that houses a thin, plastic reed that whistles when blown. The outcome is far more birdlike than the Ventrilo. You can't talk with it, but with practice your chirping will impress both avians and humans.

CUSTOMER SATISFACTION: High flying.

PLAY GUITAR IN 7 DAYS

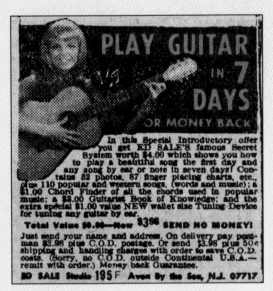

WE IMAGINED: The secret to playing guitar without all that annoying practice.

THEY SENT: Two books, a chord finder, and a pocket tuning device. The heart of the package is *Guitar Self-Taught* by Ed Sales. This sixty-four-page songbook reveals the Ed Sales secret learning method to be a series of tiny chord diagrams that appear above each line of the sheet music. He states, "The guitar chord accompaniments to the songs are shown in easy diagram form, as they are shown in all popular sheet music, enabling anyone without any previous musical knowledge to play. . . ." That's right, it's no different than any other songbook on the market.

CUSTOMER SATISFACTION: The secret method is no secret, but it works.

RIGHT: The ubiquitous diagrams.

ARCHIE CLUB

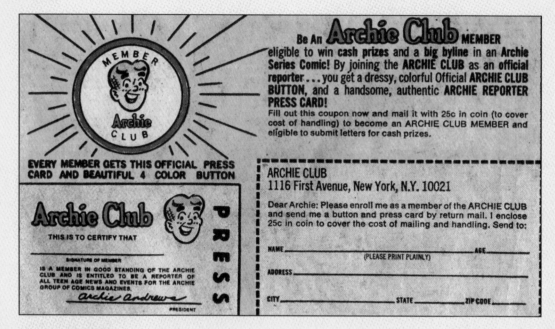

WE IMAGINED: Club membership, journalistic privileges, potential prizes, and Archie's approval.

THEY SENT: A button and a card announcing your Archie comics club membership. Anyone deputized as a "reporter of all teen age news and events for the Archie Group" became eligible to submit prose to the monthly Archie Club News feature. Card-carrying kids sent poetry, fan mail, and reports covering topics such as family pets and what they did during summer vacation. A total of five selections were published per issue. Each of them earned a cash reward, the maximum being a five-dollar first prize.

CUSTOMER SATISFACTION: Dreamy.

Count Danté

DEADLIEST MAN ALIVE

Count Danté is the undefeated Supreme Grand Master of the Fighting Arts. Count Danté won the World Overall Fighting Arts Championship (Master & Expert Divisions) after defeating the world's top Masters of JUDO, BOXING, WRESTLING, KUNG-FU, KARATE, AIKIDO, etc. in Death Matches. On Aug. 1, 1967, the World Federation of Fighting Arts crowned the Count "THE WORLD'S DEADLIEST FIGHTING ARTS CHAMPION AND MASTER."

NOW...
The World's DEADLIEST FIGHTING SECRETS Can Be Yours
· · ·

FREE ➡

BLACK DRAGON FIGHTING SOCIETY

WORLD'S DEADLIEST FIGHTING SECRETS

WE IMAGINED: A guide to becoming a deadly fighter.

THEY SENT: A brochure and a Black Dragon Fighting Society membership card. Kids who mailed an additional five dollars received the seventy-two-page booklet. The techniques are certainly deadly, but it's no secret that forcing your thumbs into a guy's eye sockets or shattering his spine could be fatal. Some of the illustrations tend to rob the book of its sophistication. However, the ferocity throughout does make the publication more engaging than the standard martial arts manual.

BEHIND THE MYSTERY: Count Danté was born John Keehan (1939–75) and became a mythical figure largely due to this ad.

CUSTOMER SATISFACTION: Lethal.

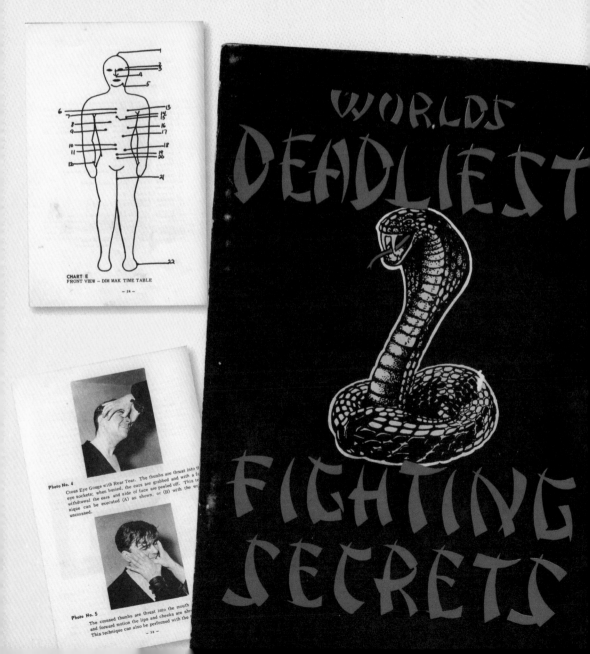

CHART E
FRONT VIEW – DIM MAK TIME TABLE

— 24 —

Photo No. 4
Cross Eye Gouge with Rear Tear. The thumbs are thrust into the eye sockets; when buried, the ears are grabbed and with a forward withdrawal the ears and side of face are peeled off. This technique can be executed (A) as shown, or (B) with the wrists uncrossed.

Photo No. 5
The crossed thumbs are thrust into the mouth and forward motion the lips and cheeks are shredded. This technique can also be performed with the

— 25 —

SECRETS OF BLACK ARTS

SECRETS OF BLACK ART

Devil's Witchcraft! Ancient magic, demonology, omens, animal magnetism, alchemy spirit & psychic phenomena, superstitions supernatural, etc. No. 1560. Price **50¢**

WE IMAGINED: An easy way to acquire nefarious, otherworldly powers.

THEY SENT: A sixty-four-page booklet that reads like a pseudo-scientific journal, rather than the step-by-step lessons in evil we were hoping for. Nevertheless, patient readers will eventually unearth practical tips, like "Any person who will wear an eelskin around his body will never have a cramp," and "If we bury a crab for three months in horse-dung, he will turn into a scorpion."

BEHIND THE MYSTERY: The hideous faces on the cover didn't originate from sacred scripts; they're actually illustrations of Halloween masks sold in early Johnson Smith catalogs. In fact, the entire second half of the book is a novelty catalog.

CUSTOMER SATISFACTION:
The magic is gone.

HERCULES WRIST BAND

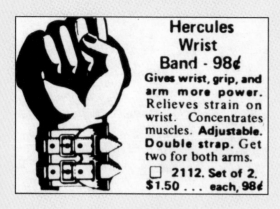

Hercules
Wrist
Band - 98¢

Gives wrist, grip, and arm more power. Relieves strain on wrist. **Concentrates muscles. Adjustable. Double strap. Get two for both arms.**

☐ 2112. Set of 2. $1.50 . . . each, 98¢

WE IMAGINED: Manly looking wrist bands sporting two metal spikes and providing heroic prowess.

THEY SENT: Leather-like wrist supports, which looked cool but lacked godly strength. What looked like spikes are really just pointed straps.

BEHIND THE MYSTERY: Superior brand wrist bands were intended for "athletes, farmers, mechanics and working men," but the savvy folks at the Johnson Smith Company remarketed them to kids by referencing the Greek hero and playing up the mighty-looking fist graphic from the box display, while wisely discarding the illustration of the bus driver.

CUSTOMER SATISFACTION: Herculean.

CHARLES ATLAS FITNESS PROGRAM

THE INSULT THAT MADE A MAN OUT OF "MAC"

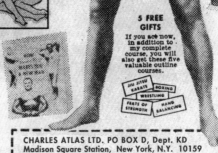

Let Me PROVE I Can Make YOU A NEW MAN!

ARE you "fed up" with seeing the huskies walk off with the best of everything? Sick and tired of being soft, frail, skinny or flabby — only HALF ALIVE? I know just how you feel. Because I myself was once a puny 97-pound "runt." And I was so ashamed of my scrawny frame that I dreaded being seen in a swim suit.

The Secret of How I Got My Build

Then I discovered a wonderful way to develop my body fast. It worked wonders for me — changed me from the scrawny "runt" I was at 17, into "The World's Most Perfectly Developed Man." And I can build up YOUR body the very same natural way — without weights, springs or pulleys. Only 15 minutes a day of pleasant practice — in the privacy of your room.

My "Dynamic-Tension" method has already helped thousands of other fellows become real he-men in double-quick time. Let it help YOU. Not next month or next year — but Right NOW!

"Dynamic-Tension" Builds Muscles FAST!

If you're like I was, you want a powerful, muscular, well-proportioned build you can be proud of any time, anywhere. You want the "Greek-God" type of physique that women rave about at the beach — the kind that makes other fellows green with envy.

Mail Coupon Now for My 32-Page Illustrated Book

Mailing the coupon can be the turning point in your life. I'll send you a copy of my 32-page illustrated book, "How Dynamic-Tension Makes You a NEW MAN." Tells how and why my method works; shows many pictures proving what it has done for others. Don't delay. Mail coupon NOW.

CHARLES ATLAS ON TV

CHARLES ATLAS

Awarded the title of "The World's Most Perfectly Developed Man."

WIN THE VALUABLE TROPHY

5 FREE GIFTS
If you act now, in addition to my complete course, you will also get these five valuable outline courses.

JIU JITSU · KARATE · BOXING · WRESTLING · FEATS OF STRENGTH · HAND BALANCING

WE IMAGINED: The key to bringing justice to a musclebound jerk in front of a dreamy girl.

THEY SENT: Charles Atlas's Dynamic-Tension® 12 Lesson Course along with an information packet inviting us to become a student of the "world's most perfectly developed man."™ Official members would receive complete bodybuilding and fitness courses that were mailed as individual lessons—such as "Health and Strength," "Food," and "Exercises for Strength and Fingers"—along with five bonus "outline courses," including "Feats of Strength" and "Hand Balancing." The program is unique in that it requires no weightlifting.

BEHIND THE MYSTERY: Charles Atlas, born Angelo Siciliano (1892–1972), experienced the sand-kicked scenario depicted in the advertisement, which prompted his interest in fitness. He was an award-winning body-builder and a Coney Island strongman before he started selling his techniques. Launched in 1929, the course is among the oldest of its kind as well as one of the most popular, boasting over 30 million students worldwide. Its iconic marketing campaign produced some of the most widely-known ads in comic book history. To this day the business continues to operate, offering the legendary fitness technique at www.CharlesAtlas.com.

CUSTOMER SATISFACTION: Healthy.

UNIVERSAL BODYBUILDING COURSE

WE IMAGINED: The path to a superhero-size body.

THEY SENT: A free brochure. Then, if you agreed to two sizable payments, you received the three-book program comprising the *Universal Abdominal Course, The Big Arm Book,* and the primary manual. As far as bodybuilding programs go, this one seems sound enough. Their dietary advice might raise a few eyebrows, however—such as the recommendation to drink seven glasses of milk and to eat two or three cans of pork and beans every day.

CUSTOMER SATISFACTION: Superman never had to work this hard.

FREE! POWERFUL MUSCLES FAST!
Fantastic New Discoveries in the science of body-building. Our method will add inches of powerful muscles to arms, chest, shoulders & legs. Learn secrets on trimming the waist with ultra-modern methods—fast! Results Guaranteed! Send for free brochure. Send 25¢ for postage and handling.

Universal Bodybuilding Box 485
Dearborn, Michigan 48121
Dept. S

FREE

Name _____ Age _____
Please Print
Street _____
City _____ State _____ Zip _____

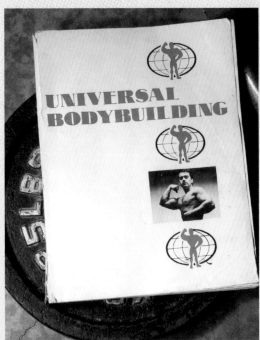

UNIVERSAL BODYBUILDING

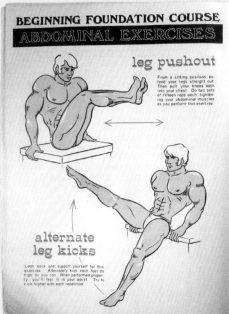

BEGINNING FOUNDATION COURSE
ABDOMINAL EXERCISES

leg pushout

From a sitting position, extend your legs straight out. Then pull your knees back into your chest. Do two sets of fifteen reps each, tightening your abdominal muscles as you perform this exercise.

alternate leg kicks

Lean back and support yourself for this exercise. Alternately kick each foot as high as you can. When performed properly, you'll feel it in your waist. Try to kick higher with each repetition.

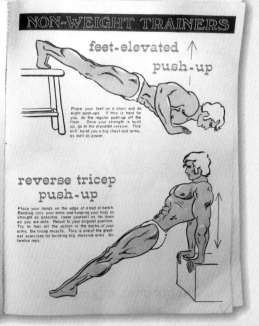

NON-WEIGHT TRAINERS

feet-elevated push-up

Place your feet on a chair and do eight push-ups. If this is hard for you, do the regular push-up off the floor. Once your strength is built up, go to the elevated version. This will build you a big chest and arms, as well as power.

reverse tricep push-up

Place your hands on the edge of a bed or bench. Bending only your arms and keeping your body as straight as possible, lower yourself as far down as you are able. Return to your original position. Try to feel all the action in the backs of your arms, the tricep muscle. This is one of the greatest exercises for building big, massive arms. Do twelve reps.

POCKET GYM

WE IMAGINED: A portable device as beneficial to our muscles as a full-size gymnasium, leading to "the admiration of the girls" in thirty short days.

THEY SENT: A twenty-inch strip of black rubber with molded handles. It's like a simplified version of the better-known, metal spring-based chest expanders, but it is safer for hairy-chested men.

CUSTOMER SATISFACTION: Wimpy.

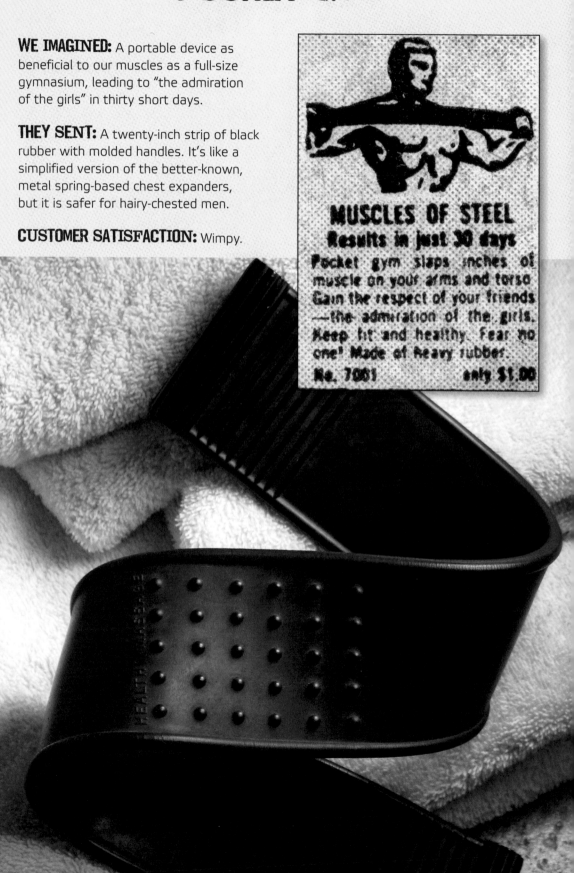

MUSCLES OF STEEL
Results in just 30 days
Pocket gym slaps inches of muscle on your arms and torso. Gain the respect of your friends —the admiration of the girls. Keep fit and healthy. Fear no one! Made of heavy rubber.
No. 7061   only $1.00

HOW TO BUILD MIGHTY MUSCLES

WE IMAGINED: A how-to guide for building mighty muscles, resulting in unbeatable self-defense.

THEY SENT: A bare-bones bodybuilding course comprising all the usual toning exercises and dumb-bell training. Ho-hum? Not with this program's unique emphasis on all the fun involved. The first page includes all of these promises: "Bodybuilding can be real fun . . . so fun-filling that you'll scarcely notice the passing of time. . . . You will realize that life can be fun and experience in full the fun of living." And, "It's fun . . . the kind of fun you get a real kick out of."

CUSTOMER SATISFACTION: Not as fun as all that.

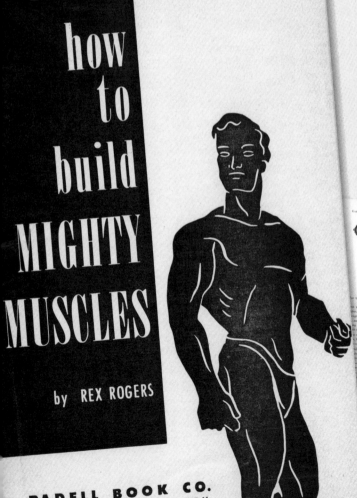

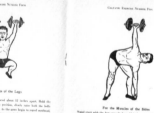

HOW TO PERFORM
STRONG MAN STUNTS

HOW TO
PERFORM
STRONG
MAN
STUNTS

AMAZE YOUR FRIENDS

Learn eleven strong man stunts which you can easily perform to astonish your audience. Book Includes He Man muscle building course--A real buy
Item #400........................50¢

HOW TO PERFORM STRONG MAN STUNTS

By
Ottley R. Coulter

PADELL BOOK CO.
NEW YORK 3

WE IMAGINED: Finally, a way to astonish audiences with our strength.

THEY SENT: A thirty-page instructional booklet from 1952 that shows us there's no need to actually become fit if you can prove your "strength" with a series of demonstrations. The eleven different stunts covered include "How to Resist the Pull of Four Men" and "How to Lift and Swing a Man with Your Teeth." The feats range from parlor tricks to physical stunts involving actual personal risk. For example, "How to Smash a Rock with a Blow of the Fist" involves soaking (and thus fatally weakening) a piece of limestone overnight, while "How to Lift a Man Overhead with One Hand" requires precisely aligning one's body for maximum leverage. Otherwise, as the book puts it, "you will fail."

CUSTOMER SATISFACTION: Smashing.

JIU JITSU—A SUPERIOR LEVERAGE FORCE

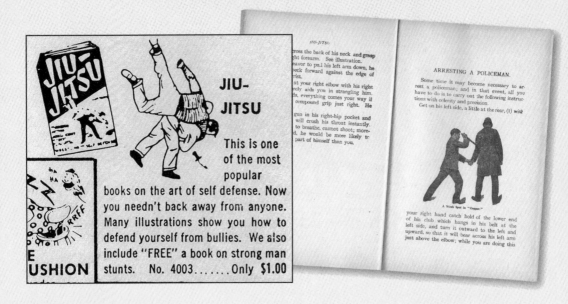

JIU-JITSU

This is one of the most popular books on the art of self defense. Now you needn't back away from anyone. Many illustrations show you how to defend yourself from bullies. We also include "FREE" a book on strong man stunts. No. 4003......Only $1.00

E USHION

WE IMAGINED: The way to achieving our standard wish list: self-defense, revenge, and admiration.

THEY SENT: *Jiu Jitsu—A Superior Leverage Force*, an uncredited booklet originally printed in 1940 yet sold decades later. On page one we learn that *Jiu Jitsu* means the "gentle art of making one's opponent use his strength to his own disadvantage." Nearly every one of its 130 pages serves up a new technique against every conceivable adversary, including boxers, wrestlers, and policemen. The last page even nonchalantly reveals the cure for the common cold: "Though it is not generally known it is nevertheless a fact that a cold which is so often caused by overloading the stomach can readily be cured by forcing pure cold air through the nostrils."

CUSTOMER SATISFACTION: Great, if you've got the sniffles.

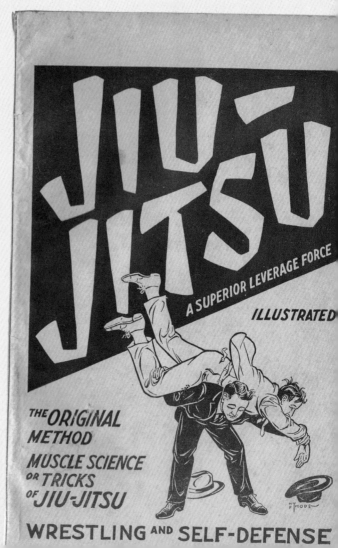

JIU-JITSU

A SUPERIOR LEVERAGE FORCE

ILLUSTRATED

THE ORIGINAL METHOD
MUSCLE SCIENCE OR TRICKS OF JIU-JITSU

WRESTLING AND SELF-DEFENSE

KETSUGO

WE IMAGINED: The ability to "reduce any assailant to cringing helplessness in seconds," learned in just one week.

THEY SENT: A manual for those tired of trying to choose between Karate, Judo, Jiu Jitsu, Savate, Aikido, Yawara, and Ate-waza. The term *Ketsugo* means combination, thus, this technique promises to provide the best of all those defenses. The many illustrations make it seem like a snap. For instance, if guy pulls a knife, you can either grab his hand, kick his hand, or kick his head. Simple.

CUSTOMER SATISFACTION: Inoffensive.

KRYPTONITE ROCKS

WE IMAGINED: A comic book prop come to life that, according to the ad, we are to posses for safe-keeping, so as to protect Superman and demonstrate our great friendship.

THEY SENT: A real rock covered in glow-in-the-dark green paint.

CUSTOMER SATISFACTION: Rock bottom.

WAR ZONE

Playtime and wartime have collided since the invention of boys. The war comic emerged as its own genre in the 1950s and achieved mainstream popularity in the 1960s and 1970s. From the beginning, mail-order dealers tantalized boys with offers of personal armies and deadly weapons for a nominal fee. Thus, armies of kids sent in a surplus of dollars, often resulting in battle-scarred expectations.

100 TOY SOLDIERS

WE IMAGINED: A massive army of war heroes. Presumably, these were cheaper but exactly the same as the ever-popular bags of soldiers that populated dime-store shelves.

THEY SENT: A cardboard box, hardly big enough to hold a grenade, containing a pile of wafer-thin warmongers. Yes, these soldiers lacked one of the three dimensions we typically look for in a toy, and each warrior scarcely contained enough plastic to make a respectable poker chip.

BEHIND THE MYSTERY: These mini GIs were the brain-children of "Uncle" Milton Levine, who was better known as the inventor of the Ant Farm. Levine read that plastic toys were expected to be big moneymakers in postwar America, so he collaborated with his brother-in-law, E. Joseph Cossman, and started a mail-order empire, originally named E. Joseph Cossman & Company.

CUSTOMER SATISFACTION: Flat.

TOY SOLDIERS

FUN TO SHOW! FUN TO COLLECT! FUN TO TRADE!

COMIC BOOK FLATS

The success of Levine and Cossman's army troops prompted numerous follow-ups, and soon a variety of companies were hawking warriors from all manner of historical conflicts. Some were competitors, but it is believed that Cossman and Levine may have set up a number of them or served as a wholesale supplier. Whether they came from Lucky Products or Helen of Toy, the soldiers maintained their underfed appearance, which prompted collectors to refer to them as "comic book flats." Their flatness is due to the fact that Milton sourced his soldiers from Nosco, the same Erie, Pennsylvania, plastics company that manufactured the equally thin Cracker Jack prizes. While the first group of soldiers were all army green, subsequent collections came in two different colors, which made battles a lot less confusing.

WWII EDITION

The WWII edition was the first of numerous soldier packs to hit the juvenile shop-at-home market. Over time the set was handled by various distributors, and the price crept well above the original one-dollar mark, but the iconic collection remained available for over forty years.

ABOVE: Footlocker design.

132 ROMAN SOLDIERS

The most famous successor is probably
the 132-piece Roman Soldier set.
This is due in part to the eye-catching
full-page battle scene featured in the ad.
The illustration was penned by renowned
comic book artist Russ Heath (*Uncanny
Tales*, *Frontline Combat*). Ironically, this
fifty-dollar art gig would become one
of Heath's best-known works.

204 REVOLUTIONARY WAR SOLDIERS

The assortment of Revolutionary Soldiers is the only one to pass the two hundred mark, making it the largest collection of its kind. This set is also notable because later versions were produced as three-dimensional figures, though they remained about half the size of store-bought soldiers. The ad bears another Russ Heath illustration.

104 KINGS' KNIGHTS

The Knights arrived in a cardboard treasure chest and were cast in black and white, making it simple to distinguish the good guys from the bad.

ABOVE: A rare look at two of the original sculpts for the set of pirates compared to the final product.

100 Little Dolls
all for $1.00

100 Dolls made of genuine Styrene plastic and hard synthetic rubber only $1 for entire set. You get BABY DOLLS, NURSE DOLLS, DANCING DOLLS, FOREIGN DOLLS, CLOWN DOLLS, COWBOY DOLLS, BRIDE DOLLS, and many more in Lilliputian cuteness. And made not of paper or rags but of STYRENE plastic and hard synthetic rubber. If you don't go wild over them your money will be promptly refunded. Send $1.00 plus 25c for postage and handling for each set of 100 Dolls you order to: 100 Doll Co., Dept. 315, 285 MARKET ST. P.O. BOX 90, NEWARK, N. J.

MAIL COUPON TODAY!

THE 100 DOLL CO., Dept. 315
285 MARKET STREET NEWARK, N. J.
Gentlemen: P. O. BOX 90
I can't wait to see if these dolls are all you say they are. Enclosed please find $............ in check ☐, money order ☐, cash ☐, for .... sets of 100 DOLLS each at $1 plus 25c for postage and handling per set. If I am disappointed in the slightest, I will send them back to you for refund as per your guarantee.
(Sorry, NO C.O.D.'s)

Name...
Address...
City.. Zone....... State.............

100 LITTLE DOLLS

As a result of the success of the mail-order soldier blitz, the format was inevitably applied to the feminine market. The 100 Little Dolls, to use the term loosely, boasted thirty different designs, giving them the highest number of unique sculpts. Styles ranged from little girls to ballerinas and, oddly enough, Santa Claus.

ATOMIC MINI PISTOL

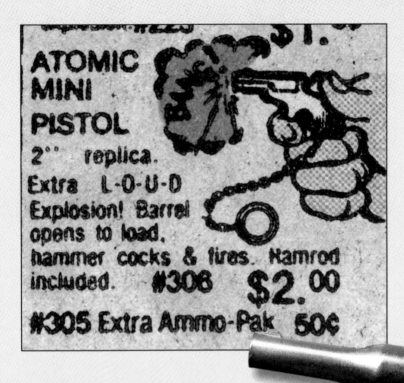

ATOMIC MINI PISTOL

2" replica. Extra L·O·U·D Explosion! Barrel opens to load, hammer cocks & fires. Ramrod included. #306 $2.00

#305 Extra Ammo-Pak 50¢

WE IMAGINED: A gun that harnesses the power of atoms (perhaps by smashing them) to create an extra-loud report.

THEY SENT: A cap gun on a key chain. It is only atomic in that it's made up of atoms. However, the product isn't a total letdown, as cap guns are inherently fun, and this one gets points for being easy to conceal. The only drawback to the size is that it loads only one cap at a time.

CUSTOMER SATISFACTION: Subatomic.

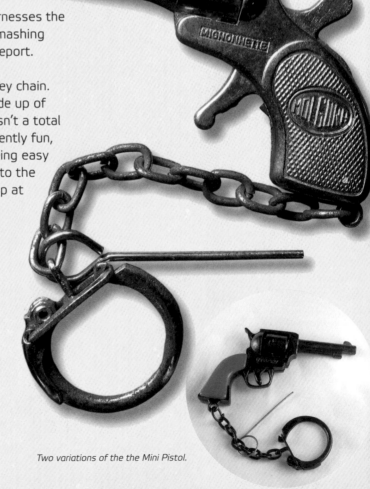

Two variations of the the Mini Pistol.

SPUD GUN

ABOVE: Eventually the metal construction was discontinued in favor of plastic.

WE IMAGINED: A gun that shoots pieces of potato.

THEY SENT: A gun that shoots pieces of potato! The Spud Gun shoots wet, starchy pellets great distances, and it instantly renews interest in the vegetables in the pantry. The only downside is discovering stray potato bullets rotting around the house.

BEHIND THE MYSTERY: The Spud Gun was an existing item made incredibly popular by mail-order guru E. Joseph Cossman. In his book *Success Secrets*, Cossman boasts about the promotional campaign that launched the craze. He asked one hundred farmers to send him five hundred pounds of free potatoes with the promise that his new toy would support farm areas nationwide. Cossman created a media-friendly spectacle by dumping the fifty thousand pounds of spuds in the streets of Manhattan. He offered the potatoes to an orphanage, and requested that they send over twenty-five orphans dressed as cowboys and Indians. The event attracted massive coverage, and Cossman sold two million guns in six months. He also takes credit for eliminating the troublesome potato surplus of 1967.

CUSTOMER SATISFACTION:
A Harvest of fun.

LOUD CARBIDE CANNON

WE IMAGINED: A very loud cannon that shoots hundreds of cannonballs.

THEY SENT: A very loud cannon that shoots nothing. The ammo, a gel called Bangsite, is made of calcium carbide and ships in a tube that produces about a hundred shots. When combined with water and a spark, it creates a satisfying 105-decibel boom, but nothing is emitted. The cannon is nine inches long and made of cast iron, which makes it one of the sturdiest and heaviest of all the comic book novelties.

BEHIND THE MYSTERY: A physics professor at Lehigh University started manufacturing Big-Bang cannons in 1912 as a safe alternative to fireworks, and they remain in production today.

CUSTOMER SATISFACTION: Shoots blanks, but still a blast.

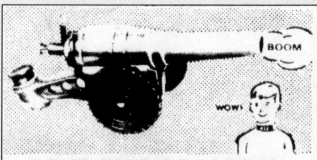

LOUD CARBIDE CANNON
Sounds like dynamite blast. Brilliant flash. Fires carbide powder ammunition. Hundreds of shots for a few cents.
X7383. Cast Iron Cannon Postpaid . . .$6.95
X7385. Ammo 60¢ Pkg.
    (500 shots). . . . . .3 for $1.50

POLARIS NUCLEAR SUB

JUL • 67

WE IMAGINED: A fully functional submarine large enough for ourself and a friend.

THEY SENT: A cardboard structure loosely resembling a submarine that would be irreparably damaged by any contact with water, including dewy grass. It includes a small mirror periscope and a built-in rubber band "torpedo" slingshot. However, the lack of mobility limits potential targets to people or animals foolish enough to pass directly in front of the sub.

CUSTOMER SATISFACTION: Sinks, then surfaces.

ABOVE: Clayton Moraga shows off his newly assembled sub.

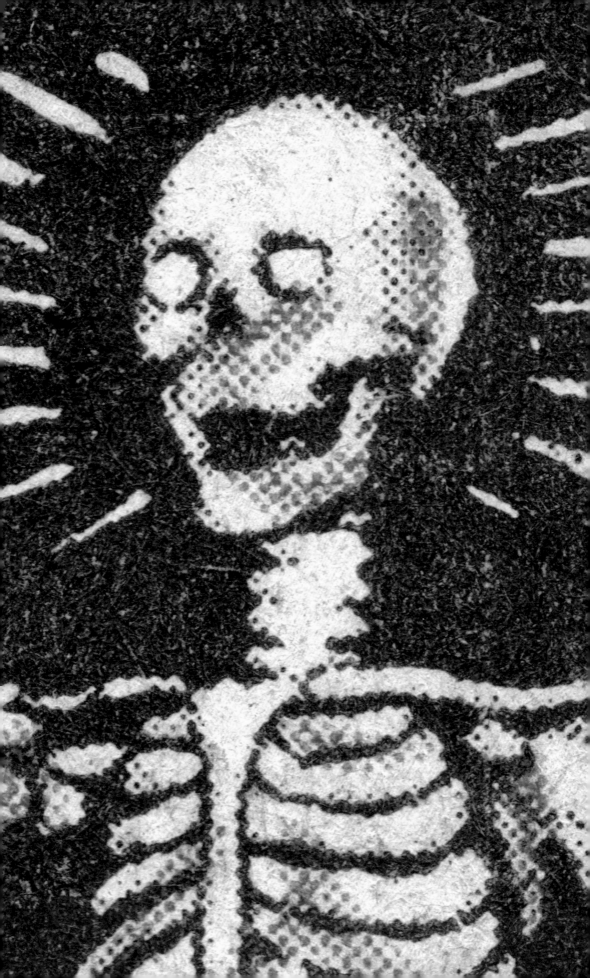

HOUSE OF HORRORS

In 1957 a bundle of early Universal horror films was syndicated to American television for the first time. The package included heavyweights like *Frankenstein*, *Dracula*, and *The Wolf Man*, and local stations were encouraged to present the material by way of a costumed "horror host." This breathed new life into the old classics and gave rise to a new generation of monster enthusiasts.

The popularity of these movies spawned the publication of *Famous Monsters of Filmland* magazine, as well as an onslaught of spooky toys, comic books, and television shows, such as *The Munsters* and *The Addams Family*. Inevitably, the mail-order industry found their place in the cultural food chain, and naturally they employed a few misleading techniques to scare up sales.

6-FOOT MONSTER-SIZE MONSTERS

WE IMAGINED: A shockingly realistic, freestanding movie monster that probably talks.

THEY SENT: A silent, yet beautifully painted six-foot poster of Frankenstein and/or Dracula. These were the first of numerous giant movie monsters to lurk in comic books and monster mags. The quality of the products and the on-the-level advertising would only diminish with time.

CUSTOMER SATISFACTION: Fun to hang up, but not to sleep next to.

In the late 1970s, a six-foot, black-and-white poster was produced based on a Frankenstein drawing by Jack Davis, a well-known commercial artist and founding cartoonist for Mad magazine.

7-FOOT MONSTER-SIZE MONSTERS

MONSTER

S·I·Z·E MONSTERS

7 FEET TALL

In Authentic Colors With **GLOW in the DARK EYES**

ONLY $1.00

TEN DAY FREE TRIAL

Just imagine your friends shock when they walk into your room and see the "Monster" reaching out—bigger than life-Frankenstein, the original man-made monster, that creation of evil genius that terrorized the world. A giant 7 feet tall, his eyes glow eerily as his hand reaches out—as aweful and sinister as the wildest nightmare. Yes—Frankenstein is 7 feet tall, in authentic colors on durable polyethelene, and so lifelike you'll probably find yourself talking to him. Won't you be surprised if he answers? Comes complete with eyes that glow even in the pitch dark for a special thrilling chill.

Boney the Skeleton. And then there is Boney—stark scary with nothing left but his bare bones. A 7 foot monster out of the grave—his bones white, his eyes staring—even **glowing in the dark.**

Money Back Guarantee.

Just send $1.00 plus 25c to cover postage and handling for each monster you want. Your money back if not satisfactorily horrified.

Honor House Dept. 205MR80
Lynbrook, N.Y. 11563

Rush me my 7 foot tall glow in the dark monsters. Send me ☐ Frankenstein ☐ Boney the Skeleton

I enclose $1 plus 25c for postage and handling for each. If I don't get shivers of delight, I can return my purchase within 10 days and you will refund the full purchase price.

NAME ....

ADDRESS ....

CITY .... STATE .... ZIP ....

New York State Residents please add sales tax.

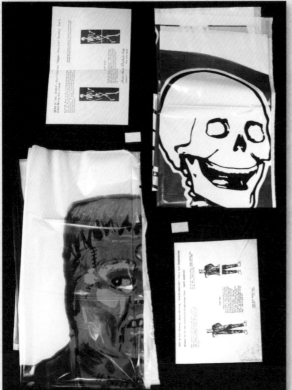

WE IMAGINED: A seven-foot action figure made of "durable polyethelene."

THEY SENT: Posters that arrived in two separate pieces, appropriately made from material similar to a trash bag. By the 1970s, Honor House dumbed down their monster art and started printing it on plastic sheets. Frankenstein's "authentic colors" became green and a darker shade of green. The glowing eyes consist of two luminous circular stickers that you apply yourself.

CUSTOMER SATISFACTION: Frankly, it's a rip-off.

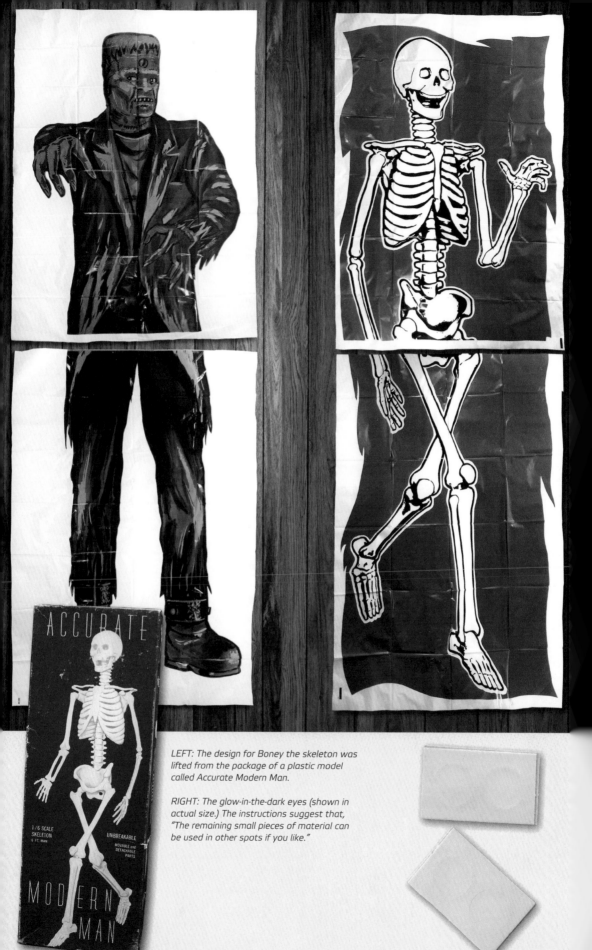

LEFT: The design for Boney the skeleton was lifted from the package of a plastic model called Accurate Modern Man.

RIGHT: The glow-in-the-dark eyes (shown in actual size.) The instructions suggest that, "The remaining small pieces of material can be used in other spots if you like."

ACCURATE

1/6 SCALE
SKELETON
6 FT. MAN

UNBREAKABLE
MOVABLE and
DETACHABLE
PARTS

MODERN
MAN

U-CONTROL 7-FOOT LIFE-SIZE GHOST

WE IMAGINED: Obviously a remote control, seven-foot-tall ghost with which to scare siblings, pets, and parents at a distance.

THEY SENT: A balloon, a spool of fishing line, and a trash bag. To make matters worse, the balloon bears the face of the decidedly unscary Casper the Friendly Ghost. The instructions outline various activities for you and your short-lived specter, including tying him to your bicycle, tying him to a kite, or filling the ghost with helium and releasing it with a note attached, advising whoever returns it that they may join your "secret society." This was a Johnson Smith exclusive until at least two other companies came up with their own versions.

CUSTOMER SATISFACTION: Haunting regret.

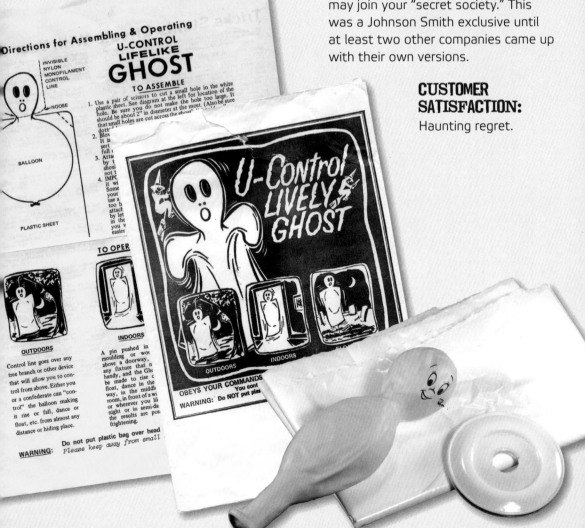

MONSTER GHOST

WE IMAGINED: An apparition that "obeys your commands," indicating internal mechanics and futuristic voice recognition technology.

THEY SENT: Not again! The envelope contains a trash bag, fishing line, and a balloon, only the Monster Ghost is slightly more terrifying than the U-Control Ghost, due to its relatively grisly skull face. The Monster Ghost arrived with four pages of instructions, though two of them reprint a loosely related short story called "The Ghost-Braham." In a rare act of decency, the instructions promise a free replacement balloon should yours burst. This spook was offered by the illusive Melton Company, who placed numerous stand-alone ads promoting it. Despite a saturated balloon-ghost market, the ruse ran for over a decade.

CUSTOMER SATISFACTION: Deflating.

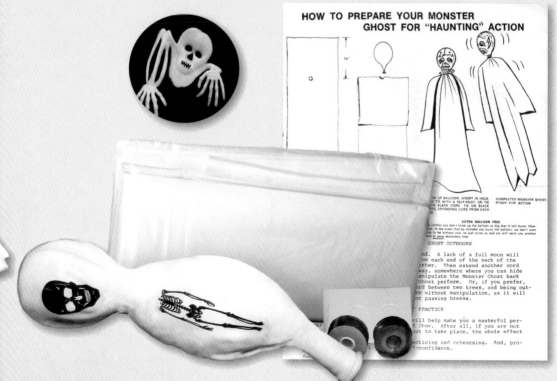

MOON MONSTER

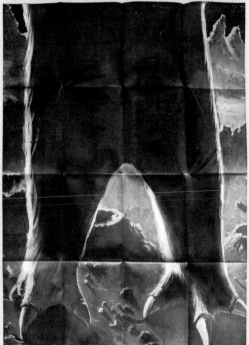

1970

HORROR FAN CLUB
Life Time Membership

_____
Members Signature

June Haley
PRESIDENT

WE IMAGINED: "A life size reproduction of a movie monster," glossy photos, a Monster Fan Club membership card, a badge, a bulletin, three monster masks, plus all the benefits and prestige that comes with membership!

THEY SENT: Two black-and-white posters that connect to form a beast that reportedly resides on the moon. Ironically, any true monster fan would recognize this brute as the titular demon from the 1957 B-movie _Curse of the Demon_. Meanwhile, the membership card says "Horror Fan Club," carelessly misnaming the very organization it supposedly represents. Most unforgivable are the bonus "monster masks," which are actually xeroxes of black-and-white photos of cheap rubber masks.

CUSTOMER SATISFACTION: Not a fan.

BOTTOM LEFT: The demon from Curse of the Demon.

RIGHT: The monster takes on a different pose in this early variation from the 1950s. Note that the two posters do not align correctly.

7 GIGANTIC DINOSAURS

giant inflatable toys of pre-historic monsters who ruled the earth millions of years ago

7 GIGANTIC DINOSAURS

WITH GENUINE TOSS-UP FEET ACTION!

MOLDED ONE-PIECE QUALITY LATEX!

COMPLETELY INFLATABLE!

for $1.00

(No COD's please)

up to 4 FEET TALL

Here's thrilling excitement for everyone with this giant-size collection of pre-historic dinosaurs at this low, low price of just $1.00 (plus post.) Thrill to their fascinating names! Command these fun-loving pre-historic monsters to your every prank! Toss them in the air and they always land on their feet . . . swinging and swaying in every direction without tilting over. Great for children! Terrific for parties! Colossal for adults! So order right now for stupendous fun. Fill out the coupon below. You take no risk because you must agree that these giant dinosaurs are everything we say or your money promptly refunded.

THEY SWING AND SWAY IN EVERY DIRECTION!

THEY BEND, LEAN, AND TILT!

EVEN THE TINIEST BREEZE ANIMATES THEM!

THEY BOUNCE AND HOP!

THEY STAND AND WIGGLE!

7 DIFFERENT PRE-HISTORIC MONSTERS IN EACH PACKAGE

CERATOSAURUS
TRACHODON
TYRANNOSAURUS REX
SEA SERPENT
DEMIHTHYS

MAIL THIS HANDY COUPON NOW!

GIANT DINOSAURS, DEPT. 86410
114 East 32nd St., New York 16, New York

I can hardly wait to get my complete collection of pre-historic dinosaurs. Please rush. Enclosed is $ in cash Money order. for postage & handling charge.

NAME
ADDRESS
CITY

INSTRUCTIONS
After inflation of balloon place mouthpiece downward thru hole in center of feet, stretch tightly back and up thru slot between feet.

WE IMAGINED: Large plastic dinosaurs made of molded one-piece quality latex, to be exact. Had we been keen-eyed enough to notice that they're "completely inflatable," we'd have guessed a beach toy.

THEY SENT: Seven balloons and some cardboard feet, which, like all balloon novelties, offer extremely limited playability. You can almost see the copywriter smirk as he or she wrote the line, "You must agree that these giant dinosaurs are everything we say or your money promptly refunded," followed by the web of masterfully worded claims.

CUSTOMER SATISFACTION: Extinct.

HOW TO DRAW MONSTERS

WE IMAGINED: Lessons for drawing monsters.

THEY SENT: A thirty-two-page booklet that teaches you, not only how to draw monsters, but how to draw, period. Art history and artists' tools and techniques are covered along with a gruesome collection of creeps. It's all presented with a healthy dose of encouragement for young pencil-bearers.

BEHIND THE MYSTERY: By the mid-1960s Harry Borgman was a well-established commercial artist whose work appeared on magazine covers and ads for General Motors. Inspired by a friend, he began contributing to a satirical humor magazine called *Sick*. In the early 1970s he delved deeper into comic book–style art for a book called *Great Tales of Horror and Suspense*. That's about the time Harry turned into Monsterman and produced *How to Draw Monsters* with the intent to sell it in comic books and magazines. It was his first book, which paved the way for a bibliography of over a dozen published works, ranging from art instruction titles to collections of his own art.

CUSTOMER SATISFACTION: In a sea of shysters, Borgman is the real deal.

GENUINE SOIL FROM DRACULA'S CASTLE

WE IMAGINED: An historic, and possibly enchanted, sample of vampire real estate presented in a classy golden coffin.

THEY SENT: A clear plastic coffin-shaped container full of what appears to be finely ground sand or perhaps nutmeg. In the ad, the apparently gold coffin turns out to be a cleverly ambiguous rendering. Would we have paid attention, the ad described it as "a transparent miniature coffin" all along. The certificate of authenticity would mean more were it not issued by Warren Publications, the same outfit that produced the ad as well as the magazine it's in.

CUSTOMER SATISFACTION: Like a stake through the heart.

Certificate of Authenticity

This is to warrant and guarantee that the soil contained in the Dracula Pendant came directly from the grounds of the authentic Castle Dracula in the Carpathian Mountains of Rumania, in the region originally known as Transylvania.

"He is as a shadow, and hath no reflection. At night, he penetrates through walls and doors. Abandon all hope, ye whom he doth approach."
from an ancient book on vampirism

The Dracula Soil Pendant was created in a limited edition of 5,000—of which this is number: N° 3059

James Warren

Warren Publishing Company Inc.
145 East 32nd Street
New York, N.Y. 10016

HORROR RECORD

WE IMAGINED: A horrifying soundtrack suitable for a multitude of frightening events, available on a convenient full-length record album.

Terrifying, Horrible sounds. Screams, moans, banshees, haunted houses, collossal thunderstorms, eerie, supernatural, horrible monsters and creatures, hideous, wild animals, maniacal laughter, many more. **Long play 33 RPM record. For parties, supernatural effects, Halloween.**
☐ **3140. Horrible Sounds Record . . . . .95¢**

THEY SENT: A low-grade recording on a thin, seven-inch record presented in a plain white sleeve. Like *The Haunting*, it plays at 33⅓ RPM and is only slightly longer, with a brief sixteen-minute run time. Side one features a by-the-numbers list of common creepy sound effects, but the real action comes on side two: here, a thinly voiced narrator offers a guided tour of a haunted castle that ends with "Krishtor the Moon Monster" destroying our entire planet. The item was a Johnson Smith Company exclusive product, although the stock audio tracks they used have shown up elsewhere, including a 1960 Halloween sound effects record called *Spook Stuff*.

CUSTOMER SATISFACTION: Grade-A entertainment, B-grade production.

THE HAUNTING RECORD

WE IMAGINED: A recording that will fool our friends into thinking they're about to be killed by ghosts.

THEY SENT: A soundtrack designed to do just that, so long as your friends are under seven. Side one is intended to be played in a pitch dark room full of children. A cheese-ball narrator announces that the deadly Blood Banshee is on the loose, followed immediately by the Banshee's howl and the sounds of a screaming boy being eaten alive. A few dead kids later, the narrator narrowly defeats the creature with a stake, and the nightmare is over.

Side two replays many of the effects used in the story, all of which sound as if they were created by one man wielding a bunch of household items. As promised, the record plays at 33⅓ RPM, but considering that each side clocks in at about five minutes, it certainly shouldn't qualify as a "long play" record. It was produced in 1971 by a mysterious short-lived company called Gayle House.

CUSTOMER SATISFACTION:
Short but scary.

BUILD YOUR OWN MONSTER PLANS

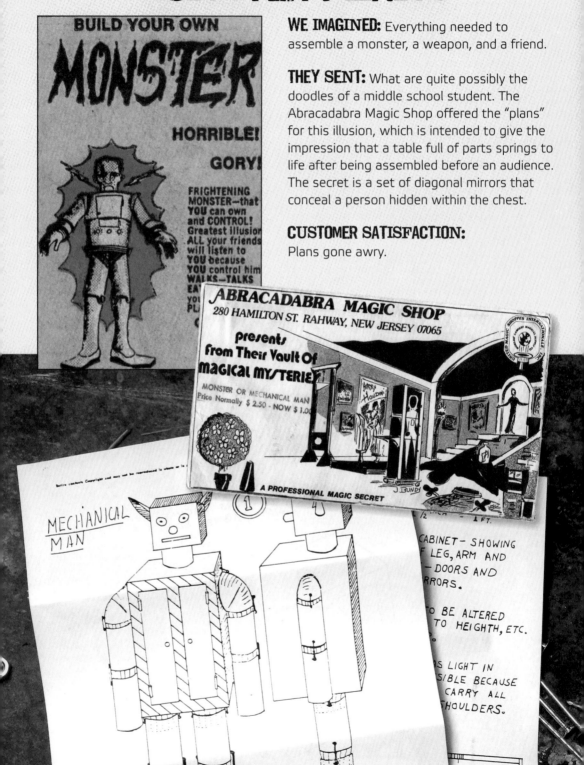

WE IMAGINED: Everything needed to assemble a monster, a weapon, and a friend.

THEY SENT: What are quite possibly the doodles of a middle school student. The Abracadabra Magic Shop offered the "plans" for this illusion, which is intended to give the impression that a table full of parts springs to life after being assembled before an audience. The secret is a set of diagonal mirrors that conceal a person hidden within the chest.

CUSTOMER SATISFACTION:
Plans gone awry.

BUILD YOUR OWN

MONSTER

HORRIBLE!

GORY!

FRIGHTENING
MONSTER—that
YOU can own
and CONTROL!
Greatest illusion
ALL your friends
will listen to
YOU because
YOU control him
WALKS—TALKS

ABRACADABRA MAGIC SHOP
280 HAMILTON ST. RAHWAY, NEW JERSEY 07065

presents
from Their Vault of
magical MYSTERIES

MONSTER OR MECHANICAL MAN
Price Normally $ 2.50 - NOW $ 1.00

A PROFESSIONAL MAGIC SECRET

MECHANICAL
MAN

CABINET — SHOWING
F LEG, ARM AND
— DOORS AND
RRORS.

TO BE ALTERED
TO HEIGHTH, ETC.

S LIGHT IN
SIBLE BECAUSE
CARRY ALL
HOULDERS.

ARM
HOLES

D LEGS TO BE MADE OF 8 INCH FURNACE
INCH STOVE PIPE.
EN SOLES

BLOODY FINGER

WE IMAGINED: A "lifelike" injured finger.

THEY SENT: Just look at it.

CUSTOMER SATISFACTION: Hacked off.

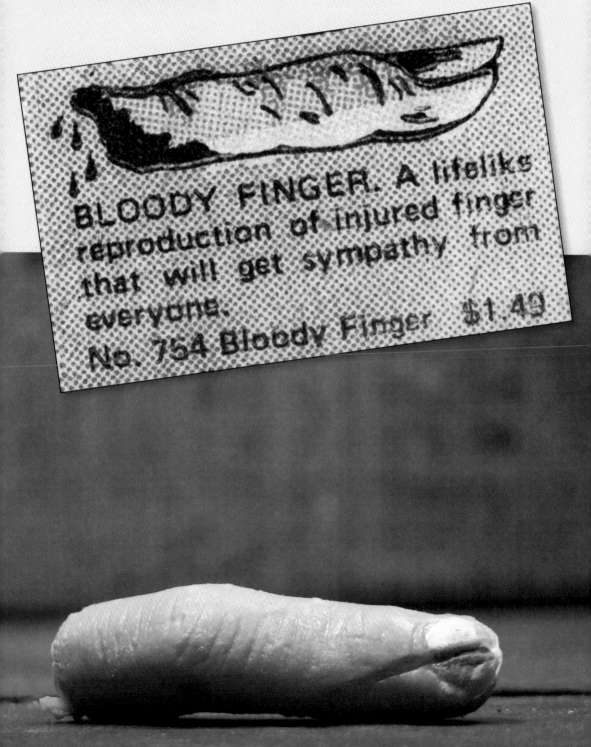

BLOODY FINGER. A lifelike reproduction of injured finger that will get sympathy from everyone.
No. 754 Bloody Finger $1.49

VAMPIRE BLOOD

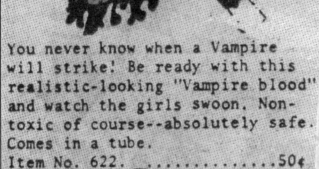

"GENUINE" VAMPIRE B-L-O-O-D

You never know when a Vampire will strike! Be ready with this realistic-looking "Vampire blood" and watch the girls swoon. Non-toxic of course--absolutely safe. Comes in a tube.
Item No. 622. ....50¢

WE IMAGINED: A pack of fake blood good for horrifying, costume-enhancement, haunted-house making, and general day-to-day use.

THEY SENT: A terrifying mixture of water, hypromellose, quaternium 15, and FD & C Red #40. The compound is more gel-like than the real thing so that it will remain in place during lengthy scaring sprees.

BEHIND THE MYSTERY: Much of the fake blood, hair, teeth, and scars available in comic books were products of Imagineering Inc. of Phoenix, Arizona. Throughout the 1970s, they advanced the business of self-horrorfication to new levels. Owner Larry Liff is credited as the creator of the very first hinged plastic fangs. The hand-drawn, hand-lettered packaging by artist Gordon Viges made their assortment irresistible then and highly collectible now. Ironically, the product's popularity skyrocketed after a false health scare involving fake vampire blood.

CUSTOMER SATISFACTION: Type A positive.

VAMPIRE BAT

WE IMAGINED: A realistic, life-size mechanical bat that produces sound and is equipped with a remote control.

THEY SENT: A small piece of molded rubber on an elastic string. While late-night monster movies taught us that bats have a two-foot wing span, this one is indeed "life-size" at about seven inches long, offering a painful lesson in biology. Promises like "Does all this at your command" were a common euphemism for a piece of string; however, one must admit that black does qualify as "authentic natural colors." The choice to overplay the bat while casually mentioning the five-piece bonus "Horror Outfit" of rubber toys is an odd one.

CUSTOMER SATISFACTION: Another fly-by-night operation.

TOPSTONE RUBBER MASKS

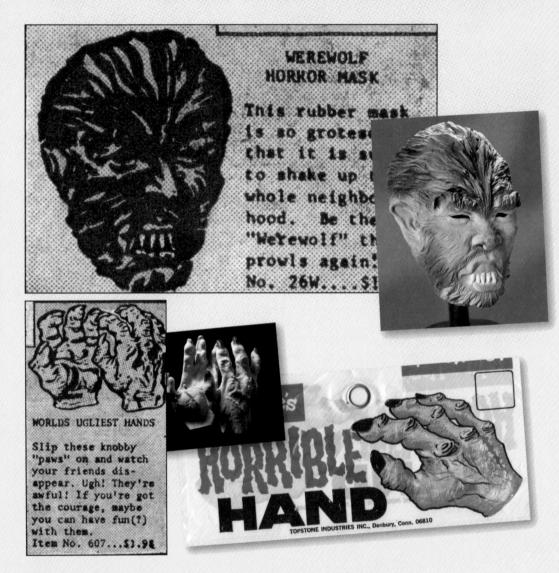

WEREWOLF HORROR MASK

This rubber mask is so grotes... that it is s... to shake up ... whole neighbor... hood. Be the ... "Werewolf" th... prowls again'... No. 26W....$1...

WORLDS UGLIEST HANDS

Slip these knobby "paws" on and watch your friends disappear. Ugh! They're awful! If you're got the courage, maybe you can have fun(?) with them. Item No. 607...$1.98

HORRIBLE HAND

TOPSTONE INDUSTRIES INC., Danbury, Conn. 06810

WE IMAGINED: The perfect way to uglify our face.

THEY SENT: A wide array of ghastly, yet budget-friendly disguises that delivered genuine thrills.

BEHIND THE MYSTERY: The Topstone Rubber Company of Bethel, Connecticut, was a costume manufacturer with a particularly strong presence in the mail-order realm. Their masks were constantly offered in the Johnson Smith lineups, and they dominated the back pages of monster magazines. Topstone masks were typically less expensive than competitors like Don Post, which made them a good candidate for allowance-earning readers.

All of Topstone's early facewear was sculpted by acclaimed artist Keith Ward (1906–2000), whose many artistic contributions include illustrating the *Dick and Jane* series of children's books. Rather than producing licensed characters, Ward reinterpreted generic creeps of all kinds. Most of the masks are stamped with a logo that says "Keith Ward Creation."

CUSTOMER SATISFACTION: Monstrous.

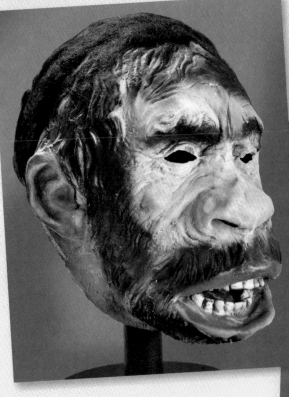

WITH
HAIR!

Rubber
Masks

"Comes To Life"

Natural, life-like, horrible!   Thin latex
rubber.   Clings when worn.   Amazingly
realistic.

☐ 4637. Wild Cave Man $3.95
☐ 4717. Savage Gorilla $3.95
☐ 4633. Realistic Frankenstein $2.95

This primitive duo started showing up in Johnson Smith ads around 1970, and they stuck together for at least a decade. The caveman was made popular by a Texas television show called Slam Bang Theater.

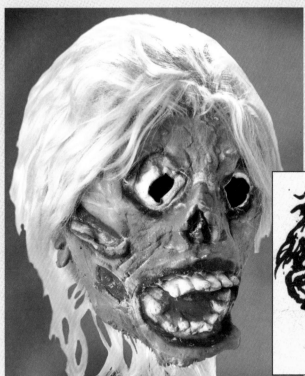

LEFT: The most famous of the bunch is arguably the Shock Monster (aka Horror Monster). Though it bears a resemblance to the creep in I Was a Teenage Frankenstein, the mask predates the film by at least one year.

SHOCK MONSTER

Eeerie green skin; black twisted hair; yellow teeth; a staring eye. Only $1.98.

GHOUL

Eerie green and yellow ghoul looks as if he just rose up out of the earth! Enlarged ears and mouthfull of horribly large teeth, plus droopy, sunken eyes make this new mask a collector's item! Only $1.49 Circle No. 11.

LAGOON MONSTER

Horrifying greenish Over-the-Head mask covers entire face; needs no elastic to keep on. Terrific shocker, with yellowish & red features. Looks just like real Hollywood kind, with lumpy skin and scales like fish. Very scary! Only $2.00. Circle No. 12 in coupon.

HORRIBLE MELTING MAN

Here's a great one! Inspired by the HOUSE OF WAX, this mask will startle anyone who sees it. Half of the face appears to be melting onto the floor! Only $1.49 Circle No. 14.

1-EYED CYCLOPS

Gruesome blue-green eye in middle of forehead; colorful, Hidden slits let you see with both your eyes. Only $1.49

MUMMY

Vivid green replica of famous Kharis Mummy; green face, rotting bandages; yellow teeth; blue-green eye sockets. Real MUMMY FAVORITE! Only $1.49.

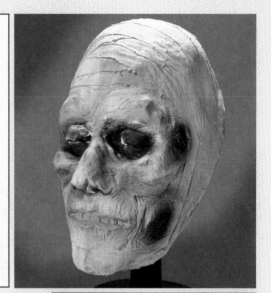

GIRL VAMPIRE

Pale white skin; long black hair; big red lips. Girls love her (boys too.) Only $1.49.

Planet Of The Apes Mask

Professionally made. Realistic in every detail. Covers full head. Realistic hair over entire head. Swollen red lips. Facial warts. Flattened nose. Deep set eyes. Clings when worn. Thin, moulded latex rubber.

☐ 4999. Deluxe Ape Man Mask. . . $12.95

RIGHT: This Planet of the Apes *mask is one of the few non-Topstone creations in the Johnson Smith catalog.*

HIGH FINANCE

Comic books have always excelled at telling kids how to spend their money. Occasionally they even offered tips on how to invest it. Mechanical banks are one solution to consider, but you've got to spend money if you want a cool place to save your money. Plus toy banks are more convenient and more fun than a real bank, unless your bank employs skeletons.

Comic advertisers also understood that get-rich-quick schemes aren't just for disillusioned grown-ups. Kids are great workhorses, and they don't expect much in return. They'll literally work for toys.

GREEDY FINGERS BANK

WE IMAGINED: A monetary storage unit with a life of its own.

THEY SENT: A cleverly designed wind-up bank that grabs your coins and makes saving fun. Coffin banks are a perennial favorite that have been around since the 1960s and are available in many varieties. At some point the lithographed tin was replaced with a plastic construction, as was the fragile felt hood.

CUSTOMER SATISFACTION: Worth the bones.

JACK POT BANK

WE IMAGINED: A bank that's also a playable slot machine.

THEY SENT: A plastic bank that only looks like a slot machine. It features spinning reels, but no coin is required to pull the lever, and there's never a payout, unless you unscrew the plug and dump your dimes on the carpet. "Not to be used for gambling" should read "Can't be used for gambling." However, it's still more addictive than a piggy bank.

CUSTOMER SATISFACTION:
The house wins again.

Jack Pot Bank
$2.95
Las Vegas Replica. 12 "winning" combinations. Insert dime, pull lever on this "One Arm Bandit" & watch the reels spin in windows to see if you have lucky winner. Realistic 5" high. Dimes are removable. Holds about $20.00. Not to be used for gambling. $2.95

☐ 3705. Jack Pot Bank $2.95

STAMPED PENNIES

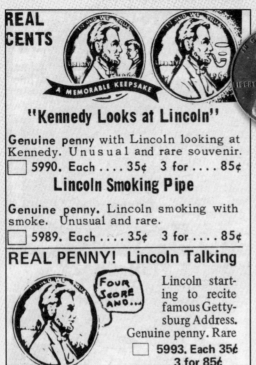

The Kennedy stamped penny includes a list of presidential coincidences as a value-add. However, many of the similarities have been debunked.

WE IMAGINED: Funny money.

THEY SENT: A common cent that was defaced and sold for fifty times its original value. The practice of creating novelty coins by stamping extraneous images in Lincoln's line of sight—as if he were smoking a pipe or offering an "I love you"—took off in the 1960s and 1970s. Like so many pointless curiosities, they swiftly found their way into mail-order ads.

BEHIND THE MYSTERY: The value of coins like these is debated among collectors. Technically they are considered damaged, but they're still worth what people will pay, and some collectors seek them out just because they're unusual. Believe it or not, there is some confusion as to whether the US mint is responsible for these. Let it be known the US treasury secretary has never signed off on a commemorative Lincoln Blowing Smoke Rings cent.

CUSTOMER SATISFACTION: Senseless cents.

GRIT NEWSPAPERS

WE IMAGINED: A solution to financial destitution and social inadequacy.

THEY SENT: Everything necessary to kick off a career in newspaper delivery. *Grit* was a reputable, weekly, tabloid-size paper that covered all the standard departments, including news, sports, classifieds, and comics.

BEHIND THE MYSTERY: *Grit's* business model relied on kids (thirteen and up) to distribute the paper across the United States. It peaked in the 1950s, when over thirty thousand kids sold more than seven hundred thousand copies a week. The publication, which was most popular in rural areas, featured conservative, optimistic journalism. Their editorial policy stated: "Do nothing that will encourage fear, worry, or temptation. . . . Put happy thoughts, cheer, and contentment into

STREET NAME PLEASING TO THE IRISH

It would be hard to think of a more fitting street name in an Irish city than that of Patrick Street in Cork. The name honors Ireland's patron saint, who is remembered every March 17 wherever there are Irishmen or persons influenced by them. In the United States, the biggest celebration is the annual parade in New York City.

[reader's] hearts." Their philosophy is exemplified in the headline seen above. Eventually, *Grit* morphed into a rural-lifestyle magazine that is still available on a bimonthly basis.

CUSTOMER SATISFACTION: It's up to you: profit or bird cage liners.

MONEY MAKER

WE IMAGINED: A device that instantly prints real money.

THEY SENT: A misrepresented magic trick. The key information conveniently missing from the ad is the fact that you must load the machine with your own money. As the knob is turned, the blank paper is rolled up inside some black fabric while preloaded bills are fed out the other side. A few of the more scrupulous dealers had the decency to mention the word "illusion" in the write-up, but most did not. Many kids saw this ad and formed the same plan: save enough cash to buy this item, then print enough money to buy everything else. It was like asking a genie for a million more wishes.

CUSTOMER SATISFACTION: The great depression.

THE MONEY MAKER

Put in a blank piece of paper, turn the knob... out comes a REAL dollar bill! You can spend it! Makes $5's, $10's, $20's & more! A mystifying trick! Order YOURS TODAY! Only $1.25

MONEY CHANGER

MONEY CHANGER
Just like a professional money changer, Attaches to any belt, Holds pennies, nickels, dimes and quarters.
No. 70 $1.25

WE IMAGINED: A change dispenser that attaches to our belt "just like a professional money changer."

THEY SENT: Exactly that, giving you the power to aid crowds of desperate bill holders in dire need of change for a parking meter or a vending machine. Only you, the human jackpot, can save them.

CUSTOMER SATISFACTION: Fun as a professional money changer, guaranteed.

SALES PROGRAMS FOR KIDS

LEFT: Christmas card sample book and prize catalog from the Sales Leadership Club.

WE IMAGINED: Filling our bedrooms with loads of new goodies.

THEY SENT: Samples of stuff you had to sell.

BEHIND THE MYSTERY: For decades comic books were jammed with ads from organizations like Youth Opportunity Sales Club, Sales Leadership Club, and American Specialty Co.—all seeking underaged professionals to move things like plaques, seeds, and lots and lots of greeting cards. Their common approach was a full-page ad brimming with toys, sporting goods, bikes, and electronics, but where you'd normally see prices,

they listed the sales requirements to earn each item.

Generally speaking, these programs were aboveboard. They delivered on their promises, and the rewards were no more shoddy than the products found in department stores. Naturally it didn't pan out for many, but a surprising number of former pint-size participants attribute their entrepreneurial success as adults to the early business lessons they learned with these programs.

CUSTOMER SATISFACTION:
If you didn't get a bike, it's your own fault.

ABOVE: Boxed Christmas cards offered by the Junior Sales Club of America and the official JSCA badge.

TOP LEFT: Olympic Sales Club official membership card.
LEFT: A package of seeds from the American Seed Co.
ABOVE: A metal Social Security plate.

FREE ONE MILLION CASH

Fool all yours friends. You'll get a Million $$$ worth of laughs with these exact reproductions of old U. S. Gold Banknotes (1840). They're yours FREE when you send for our brand new "FUN CATALOG." Send only 35c (coin) for shipping.

THE FUN HOUSE
BOX 1225-MC• NEWARK. N. J. 07101

WE IMAGINED: A sack of play money.

THEY SENT: A single reproduction US Gold Banknote from 1840. Unfortunately, it's not nearly as fun as a plump sack with a dollar sign, but it was free, and it did come with a catalog. The parchment and the printing is authentic-looking enough to make this the trick that keeps on tricking. To this day, "lucky" people are still finding these in attics and drawers and briefly hoping that their financial worries have come to an end.

CUSTOMER SATISFACTION:
Worth every cent.

THE FUN HOUSE
P. O. BOX 1225
NEWARK, NEW JERSEY 07101

Bulk Mail
U.S. Postage
PAID
Newark, N.J.
Permit No. 5096

here's your

FUN CATALOG

Magic Tricks · Toys & Novelties · Souvenirs, etc.

BETTER LIVING THROUGH MAIL ORDER

Comic books offered kids the tools to enhance and streamline nearly every aspect of life. The selections ranged from strictly utilitarian objects like pocket calculators to purely frivolous concerns such as pocket games. Some products seamlessly combined both qualities: a comb that opens like a switchblade, or a light-up, robot-shaped pen. The assortment was particularly alluring because few of these items ever turned up at the local shopping center. Through years of trial and error, the mail-order pros landed on a collection of items that appealed specifically to armchair shoppers. Unfortunately, this was often because given the chance to examine the stuff in a store, nobody would ever buy it.

SILENT DOG WHISTLE

WE IMAGINED: The power to control the canine kingdom, or at least tilt a dog's head.

THEY SENT: A dog whistle of questionable effectiveness. Surprisingly, this model is not even entirely silent, as it produces an audible, albeit weak whistle. Results of a neighborhood dog test were inconclusive. It didn't provoke any noticeable reaction, let alone the confused-looking tilted dog head response that was desired.

CUSTOMER SATISFACTION: Less effective than "Here, Spot!"

Item No. 622

SILENT DOG WHISTLE

This whistle can't be heard by human ears, but Rover can hear it half a mile away. Your dog will understand that this whistle is for him alone. Be amazed how quickly he responds.
No. 701 ....$1.00

WALK-A-MATIC

WE IMAGINED: An electronic device that calculates how far we walk, quantifying the distance of our jaunt to school or even a full day's total.

THEY SENT: A mechanical pedometer that does work "with some accuracy," as the instructions state. The mechanism registers the regular movements of your body as it rises and falls with each step, and it displays your progress in quarter-mile increments viewed through four windows. The correct window for your distance is determined by your stride length. Although imprecise, the crude mechanics emulate the digital pedometers of today.

CUSTOMER SATISFACTION: Incremental.

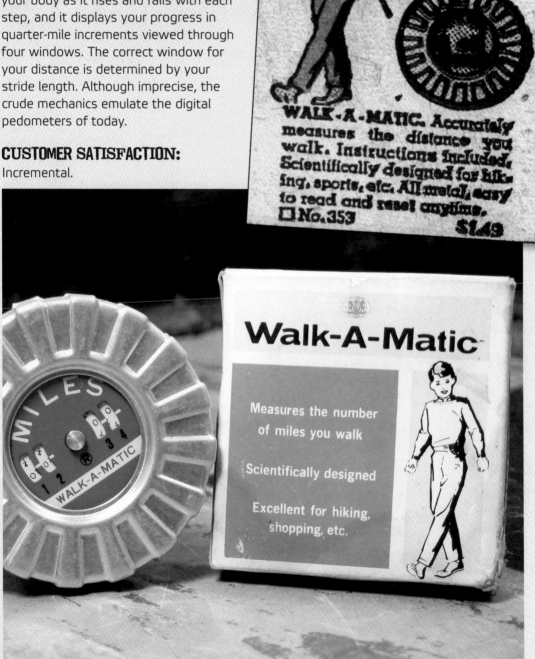

WALK-A-MATIC. Accurately measures the distance you walk. Instructions included. Scientifically designed for hiking, sports, etc. All metal, easy to read and reset anytime.
☐ No. 353 $1.49

Walk-A-Matic

Measures the number of miles you walk

Scientifically designed

Excellent for hiking, shopping, etc.

MAGIC ART REPRODUCER

WE IMAGINED: A handy gadget that projects whatever is in front of us onto a sheet of paper, enabling us to draw girls in swimsuits really well.

THEY SENT: A seven-inch-tall metal device that does not work the way it appears to. Despite the luminous-looking lines in the illustration, there's no light, and no image is projected. The artist must hunch over the little black box and squint through a peephole the size of a BB in order to see a faint image of their model that is reflected by a mirror onto a tilted piece of glass within. As long as you peer through the viewing hole, your subject's subtle reflection appears superimposed over the drawing paper, where it can theoretically be traced. It's tough to do and almost impossible not to bump the whole unit out of position. The

size of each drawing is limited to an area of about five square inches, and the art reproducer requires a darkened room. Yes, the instructions specify that your subject should be well lit while "a minimum of light falls on your drawing paper."

CUSTOMER SATISFACTION:
Thou art a rip-off.

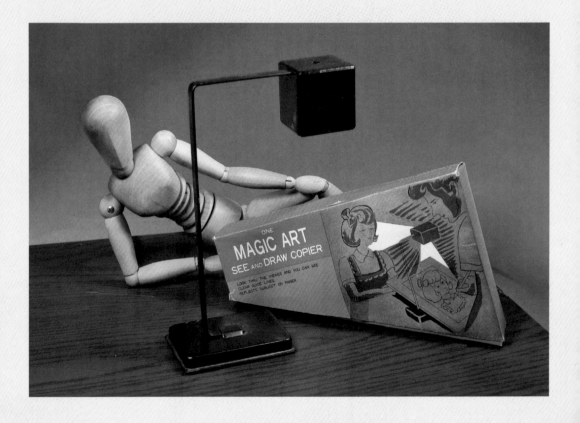

RAQUEL WELCH PILLOW

RAQUEL WELCH PILLOW

ONLY $1.98 What man wouldn't enjoy spending a night with Raquel Welch? Well, we can't deliver her, but we can deliver that next best thing —a 12" x 24" inflatable pillow of Raquel made of rugged vinyl to serve as your headrest. Keep her for yourself or show her to your friends. Livens up party when everyone sees and feels this great gag item.

RR15. . . . $1.98

ALGER BROOKLYN, N.Y. U.S.A.

WE IMAGINED: A soft, huggable, kissable pillow.

THEY SENT: A vinyl, inflatable pillow that's not as large as one you would sleep on. To be fair, this was spelled out right in the ad. A pillowcase may have been more practical because this Raquel is cold, glossy, and vulnerable to sharp objects.

CUSTOMER SATISFACTION: Not the perfect date, still fun to hang out with.

1001 THINGS YOU CAN GET FREE

FREE SAMPLES BOOKS, STAMPS, ETC.

Over 1001 Free Items Yours for the Asking

Imagine! This unbelievable book (a big 64 pages) actually tells you where to write for hundreds of $$$ worth of free items by simply writing and asking. There's no catch to it . . . you receive valuable samples, coins, foreign stamps, books, how-to-manuals, etc. . . . fabulous free items for children, teens, men, women — everyone.

Order No. TF1000 50¢

"Complete Writing Kit" includes 64 pg. Things Free Book, (2) Pens and pre-printed $1

WE IMAGINED: So much free stuff that our mailbox resembles a giant cornucopia overflowing with beautifully wrapped packages like the one on the book's cover.

THEY SENT: A sixty-four-page booklet that lacks the dictionary-thickness depicted in the ads. This edition is indispensable for anyone craving safety tips and product information. Roughly 85 percent of the freebies are pamphlets with titles like: "How Paper Came to America," "How Shall I Tell My Daughter," "Let's Collect Shells and Rocks!" and "Your House Is on Fire."

A handful of items are worth noting: a six-inch plastic ruler, trick candles, a roll of film, and sample packets of Sweet'N Low, all totally free! Actually, most items require a self-addressed stamped envelope in addition to your initial postage. Plus, of course, you have to pay for the booklet.

CUSTOMER SATISFACTION: You get what you pay for.

MINI SKULL FLASHLIGHT

WE IMAGINED: The most useful plastic skull ever conceived—thanks to a hidden button only we can operate.

THEY SENT: A light-up skull key chain with a "secret button" that's as hidden as a doorknob.

CUSTOMER SATISFACTION: Light-headed.

MINI SKULL FLASHLIGHT Lights at touch of SECRET button. FREE key chain. Battery included. #952 $1.00

ABOVE: The secret button.

STRAT-O-MATIC BASEBALL GAME

WE IMAGINED: Some sort of thrilling baseball game.

THEY SENT: Cards full of player statistics. Dice rolls are cross-referenced with the charts on the cards to determine the outcome of each play. The stats provided are based on players' real-life seasonal performances, which lends a surprisingly high level of realism.

BEHIND THE MYSTERY: Strat-O-Matic was developed in 1961 by a Bucknell University mathematics student named Hal Richman. The game attracted an avid fan base and influenced modern-day fantasy baseball leagues and other strategy card games like Magic: The Gathering. The Strat-O-Matic company is still in business, and the game has been translated into a computerized version.

CUSTOMER SATISFACTION: RBI meets RPG.

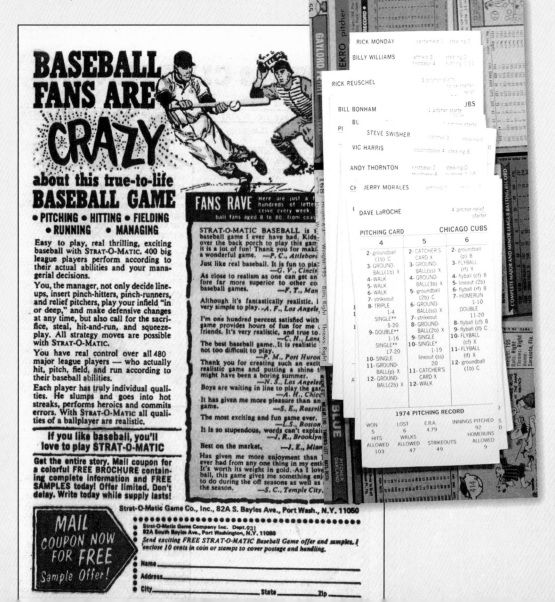

HIGH SCHOOL RING

WE IMAGINED: A handy way to fool people into thinking you're older or more educated than you really are.

THEY SENT: A cheap, generic version of a class ring that simply says "High School" in lieu of an actual institution, and the sides feature bald eagles rather than a specific sport or area of study. The ruse could turn ugly if others start asking questions, so one hopes that people will see it and silently admire your achievement.

CUSTOMER SATISFACTION: C+

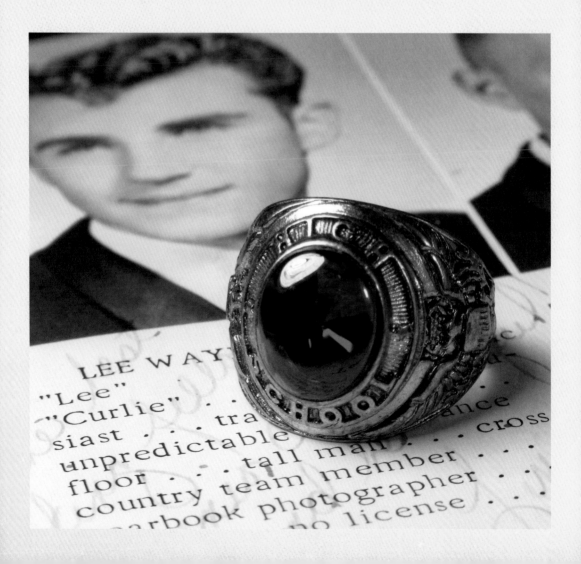

CYLON RAIDER LITE WRITER

WE IMAGINED: A light-up ink pen shaped like a Cylon Raider—a must for fans of the *Battlestar Galactica* TV show who write in dark places!

THEY SENT: A Cylon Raider Lite Writer not unlike the one pictured. Obtaining this promotional premium required three Boyer's candy wrappers. If the brand wasn't carried in your town, there was still a slim chance of finding a store that sold the extended line of Lite Writers, which included characters like Smurfs, Flash Gordon, and DC Comics' Superheroes.

CUSTOMER SATISFACTION: Bright.

MAGIC BRAIN CALCULATOR

WE IMAGINED: A handheld, bargain-priced electronic calculator.

THEY SENT: A glorified abacus. To operate the "magic brain," you must stick the point of the metal stylus into tiny slots that correspond to each number and drag them up or down (or up, over to the left, and down) depending on the color of the slot. The gadget is somewhat ingenious, but as the instructions warn, "It takes practice." There was a time when machines like the Magic Brain Calculator were indispensable. However, by the 1970s, the term calculator was synonymous with battery-operated portables from the likes of Casio and Texas Instruments. The ambiguous drawing in later ads only supported this misconception.

CUSTOMER SATISFACTION: Doesn't add up.

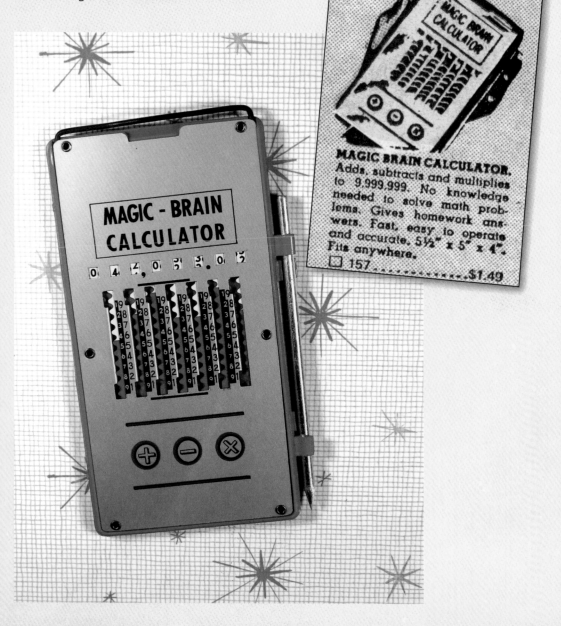

MAGIC BRAIN CALCULATOR. Adds, subtracts and multiplies to 9,999,999. No knowledge needed to solve math problems. Gives homework answers. Fast, easy to operate and accurate. 5½" x 5" x ¼". Fits anywhere.
☐ 157................$1.49

SWITCHBLADE COMB

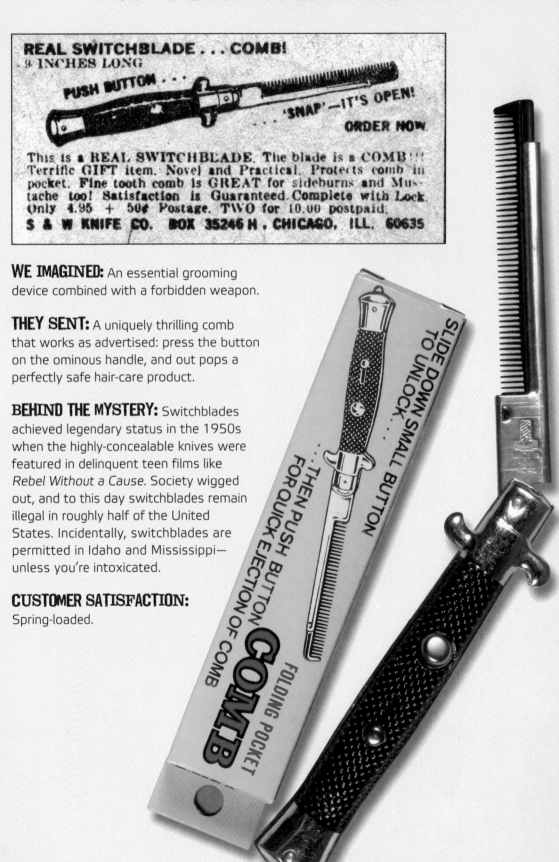

WE IMAGINED: An essential grooming device combined with a forbidden weapon.

THEY SENT: A uniquely thrilling comb that works as advertised: press the button on the ominous handle, and out pops a perfectly safe hair-care product.

BEHIND THE MYSTERY: Switchblades achieved legendary status in the 1950s when the highly-concealable knives were featured in delinquent teen films like *Rebel Without a Cause*. Society wigged out, and to this day switchblades remain illegal in roughly half of the United States. Incidentally, switchblades are permitted in Idaho and Mississippi— unless you're intoxicated.

CUSTOMER SATISFACTION: Spring-loaded.

SLIDE DOWN SMALL BUTTON TO UNLOCK . . .

. . . THEN PUSH BUTTON FOR QUICK EJECTION OF COMB

FOLDING POCKET **COMB**

VACUTEX BLACKHEAD REMOVER

WE IMAGINED: The solution to clear skin, a prerequisite to romance.

THEY SENT: A plastic apparatus that produces a mild suction through a hole in the tip when the handles are retracted. Any unpleasantness that is extracted is ejected by a plastic rod inexplicably called a "direction finder."

CUSTOMER SATISFACTION: Skin deep.

Ugly Blackheads—Out in Seconds

Keep your complexion free of black heads- look attractive instantly. Scientifically designed vacuum pump gently "lifts" out ugly blackheads safely. No pinching or squeezing. Made in U.S.A.—beware of imitations. Try 10 days—if not delighted return for refund. Send $2 plus 25¢ pstg. & hdlg. **BALLCO PROD. CO., INC.** **191 MAIN ST., DEPT. 310-A, WESTPORT, CONN. 06881**

VACUTEX

JET "ROCKET" SPACE SHIP

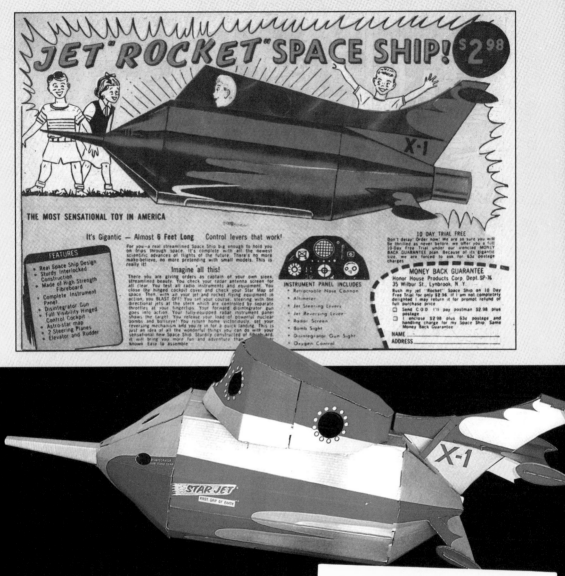

WE IMAGINED: A rocket big enough to sit in made of "brightly colored fiberboard," whatever that is.

THEY SENT: A huge cardboard rocket ship. The phrase "Control levers that work!" would be more accurate if it was "Control levers that move!" And "going forward and backward, banking left and right" should have read "sits totally still."

CUSTOMER SATISFACTION: Still more fun than a cardboard box.

50 BIKE DECALS

WE IMAGINED: An affordable way to spruce up our bike.

THEY SENT: An assortment of small water-transfer decals that were a veritable encyclopedia of coolness.

BEHIND THE MYSTERY:
Throughout the mid-twentieth century, a New Jersey outfit called Impko beautified the United States with portable, eye-popping graphics that were printed on postcards, pennants, bumper stickers, patches, and lots and lots of decals. Their specialties were travel souvenirs and imagery inspired by the hot rod "Kustom Kulture" of the 1960s. Impko's vast selection included art from Rat Fink creator Ed "Big Daddy" Roth, as well as their own original monsters, animals, skulls, flames, girls, and anything else that looked good on a roadster.

CUSTOMER SATISFACTION:
Lookin' good.

AIR CAR HOVERCRAFT

WE IMAGINED: A working hovercraft, probably a toy, but maybe life-size.

THEY SENT: A twelve-inch battery-operated toy that actually floats on air, even over water. The Air Car houses a propeller that blows downward and lifts the hollow body. The main drawback is that it's impossible to steer, and the controller is connected by a five-foot cord, a detail left out of the ad.

BEHIND THE MYSTERY: Also known as the Scoot, the Air Car was a product of the Victor Stanzel Company, a well-established manufacturer of flying model airplanes.

CUSTOMER SATISFACTION: Stays afloat.

9-FOOT HOT AIR BALLOON

WE IMAGINED: A hot air balloon, definitely large enough to carry you and a friend.

THEY SENT: Some string, some wire, and a whole lot of colored tissue paper. The first step is to follow the cryptic instructions on how to glue together the tissue to form a giant balloon. Step two involves building a fire and funneling the hot air through a stove pipe (not supplied), though it's not likely that many kids ever made it to step two.

CUSTOMER SATISFACTION: Tempers will rise.

9-FT. HOT AIR BALLOON
9-FOOT TALL

Rises to amazing heights on just hot air. Safe as no flames are carried aloft. Use it over & over. Will carry parachutes, cameras. Multi-colored, precut gores. Complete kit & instructions for inflating, launching. Only $2.00 postpaid or 2 for $3.50. Send cash, check, or money order to—

ONLY 2.00

SPACE AGE DISTRIBUTING CO.
Dept AB
Money Back 421 Fontenelle, S.E.
Guarantee. Grand Rapids, Mich. 49508

SPACE AGE DIST
8241 STONEY
CHAGRIN FALLS, OHIO 44023

SPACE AGE DISTRIBUTING CO.
4888 CEDAR RIDGE N.E.
GRAND RAPIDS, MICHIGAN 49505

THE ORIGINAL
SPACE AGE
HOT AIR BALLOON

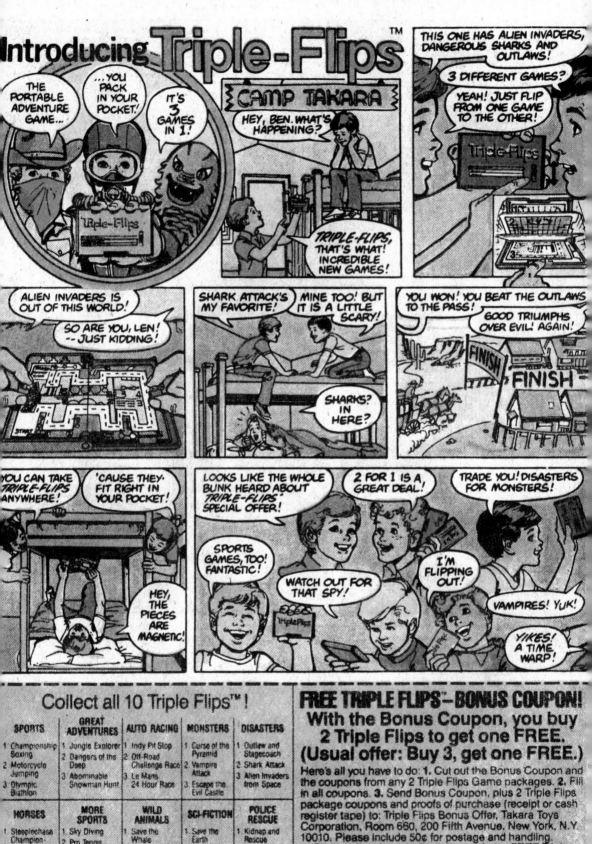

TRIPLE-FLIPS

WE IMAGINED: A portable three-in-one gaming system that includes toylike playing pieces.

THEY SENT: A plastic case that opens to one of three playing fields depending on where you position the slider. The pieces are nondescript colored tokens, although they are conveniently magnetized. The games themselves are so simplistic that popping open the case to reveal the different boards can be more entertaining than playing them.

CUSTOMER SATISFACTION: You might not flip, but it's not a flop.

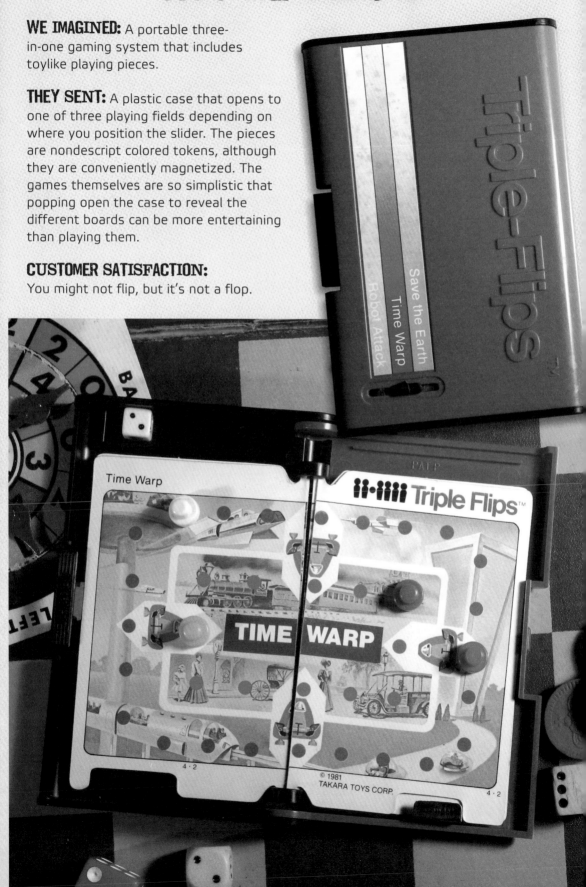

TOP SECRET

Espionage has been popular in fiction since the days of Sherlock Holmes, but a handful of television shows made the subject especially attractive to kids of the 1960s, including *The Man from U.N.C.L.E.*, *Get Smart*, and *I Spy*. It was an easy sell; few things create youthful excitement like being in on a secret, and most kids are already experts on sneaking around. As we all know, a good spy is nothing without an arsenal of gadgets. That's where novelty salesmen stepped in.

ELECTRONIC LIE & LOVE DETECTOR

WE IMAGINED: A scientifically accurate tool to identify who loves you and who's lying.

THEY SENT: A battery-operated contrivance that appears to gauge something, but with apparently random results. Two metal terminals attached to wires are placed in the hands of a couple to supposedly measure their love. When applied to an individual, the device is said to reveal lies. Movement of the needle in the readout window is supposed to indicate the intensity of the romance or the severity of deceit, respectively. In modern-day tests, the needle showed very limited activity no matter how intensely the subjects lied, or loved.

BEHIND THE MYSTERY: The Love Tester was released in 1969 by Nintendo, the same company that would build an empire on a digitized Italian plumber. There is cause to suspect that the "lie" function was tacked on to the ads and instructions by the Johnson Smith Company to give it wider appeal.

CUSTOMER SATISFACTION: Uncharted.

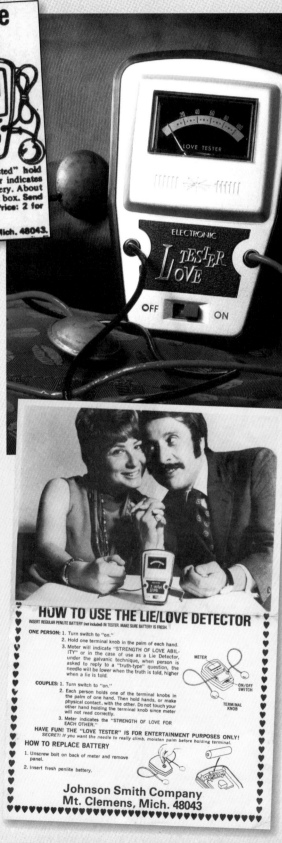

HOW TO USE THE LIE/LOVE DETECTOR

INSERT REGULAR PENLITE BATTERY (not included) IN TESTER. MAKE SURE BATTERY IS FRESH.

ONE PERSON:
1. Turn switch to "on."
2. Hold one terminal knob in the palm of each hand.
3. Meter will indicate "STRENGTH OF LOVE ABILITY" or in the case of use as a Lie Detector, under the galvanic technique, when person is asked to reply to a "truth-type" question, the needle will be lower when the truth is told, higher when a lie is told.

COUPLES:
1. Turn switch to "on."
2. Each person holds one of the terminal knobs in the palm of one hand. Then hold hands, or make physical contact, with the other. Do not touch your other hand holding the terminal knob since meter will not read correctly.
3. Meter indicates the "STRENGTH OF LOVE FOR EACH OTHER."

HAVE FUN! THE "LOVE TESTER" IS FOR ENTERTAINMENT PURPOSES ONLY!
SECRET! If you want the needle to really climb, moisten palm before holding terminal.

HOW TO REPLACE BATTERY
1. Unscrew bolt on back of meter and remove panel.
2. Insert fresh penlite battery.

Johnson Smith Company
Mt. Clemens, Mich. 48043

SECRET BOOK SAFE

SECRET BOOK SAFE
Looks like real book but opens to reveal combination lock safe.
#660
$2.95

WE IMAGINED: A secure and practical way to protect our allowance.

THEY SENT: A bank that might pass as a book at a glance, though it's about half the size of the average best seller. Technically, the lock does function, but the real flaw lies in the construction: Any kid sister could demolish the pasteboard casing with ease.

CUSTOMER SATISFACTION:
We were robbed.

SECRET BOOK SAFE WITH COMBINATION LOCK

KINGSOPLASTIC

CODE
1. CLEAR DIAL BY TURNING 4 TIMES TO THE RIGHT STOPPING AT '0'.
2. TURN DIAL TO THE LEFT STOPPING AT '16'.
3. AFTER CAREFULLY DIALING THE ABOVE COMBINATION SLIDE DOWN THE DIAL AND PULL TO OPEN.

NO. 532. MADE IN HONG KONG

BINOCULAR EYEGLASSES

SUPER POWER-VISION

POWERFUL BINOCULAR EYEGLASSES

The binoculars you wear like eyeglasses! Rugged, strong, yet so light. Provide new fun for, baseball, football, hunting. movies and T.V. Comparable to models selling at $3.95 Now yours for only $ 1.⁰⁰ 2 for $1.75

WE IMAGINED: Binoculars you wear on your face, eliminating wasted energy from all that lifting.

THEY SENT: Especially weak glasses-style binoculars. The slight magnification is roughly the equivalent of standing ten feet closer to your subject. To be fair, if the plastic lenses were any more substantial, gravity would yank the glasses from your face.

CUSTOMER SATISFACTION: Less-than-spectacular spectacles.

SPECTACLE BINOCULAR

MADE FOR CHADWICK MILLER IN HONG KONG

10-IN-1 SCOPE

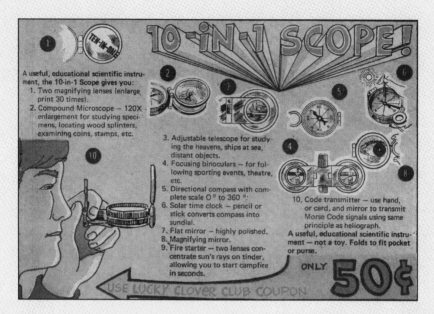

WE IMAGINED: A multifunctional viewing apparatus enabling us to see things better far and near. Not to mention a signaling mirror that could save our life or help us remove debris from our eye.

THEY SENT: An inventive little invention that more or less does what it says. There are a few factors to criticize: the flimsy construction, the suspicious claim that the microscope enlarges 120 times, and the way they call it a telescope when you look through one half of the binoculars. Most of the functionality isn't necessary for everyday life, so the moment it arrives you may wish you were lost in the woods, where it would really come in handy.

CUSTOMER SATISFACTION: Ten to one it'll come in handy.

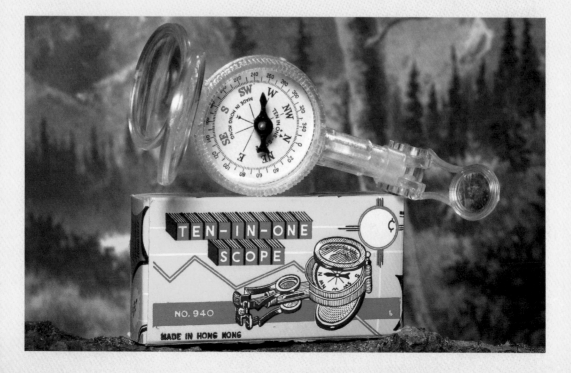

SECRET SPY SCOPE

Pen Size—Clips On Your Pocket-6-Power Magnifier. This exciting new 6-power wide field magnifier is cleverly concealed in a pen-sized pocket scope that lets you "peek" to your hearts content. So handy for Sporting Events, Counter-spying and Girl Watching. Also contains a 30-power full microscope to thrill any naturalist. Not a toy, but a real instrument. Full money back guarantee if not delighted.

Secret Spy Scope

ONLY $1..98

Item No. F59 $1.98

WE IMAGINED: A discreet way to watch girls while remaining undetected.

THEY SENT: A pocket telescope that magnifies to a reasonable extent. However, as you hold it to your eye, the view of distant objects is purpose-defeatingly shaky. Some versions of the ad seem to suggest a metal construction, but the real thing is made of plastic.

CUSTOMER SATISFACTION: Outlook not so good.

SPY WATCH

Secret Weapon "Spy Watch"

Shoots Pellets! Looks like real watch, but is actually a pellet firing mechanism. Simply load pellet, push side button & ZING! Virtually impossible to detect source of shot. Fits most wrists. Durable plastic.

9099. Spy Watch.......... $1.00

WE IMAGINED: A pellet launcher that "looks like a real watch."

THEY SENT: While the obvious sticker on the face isn't fooling anyone, the device does shoot, which provides a universal, inexhaustable appeal. However, it is only inconspicuous if the kid wearing it usually sports a bulky, men's wristwatch.

CUSTOMER SATISFACTION: Intrigue-ing.

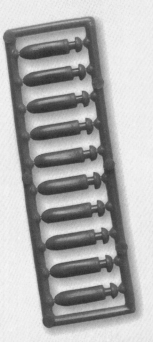

SECRET AGENT SPY CAMERA

SECRET AGENT SPY CAMERA. Easily concealed in the palm of your hand. Takes secret or surprise pictures as well as regular candid shots. Solid all metal construction. Precision ground lenses. Speed, 1/25th of a second and time exposure. Takes 10 pictures per roll.

☐ No. 109
Camera only $1.00
☐ No. 112 Hi Speed
          6 rolls $1.00

WE IMAGINED: A covert method of photographing enemy agents, i.e. girls.

THEY SENT: A tiny functional camera stripped down to its basic essentials: a lens, a shutter, and a dark place for the film. Well, mostly dark; these cameras are notorious for leaking light. The unusual size is good for spying but requires miniature, hard-to-find film. The lack of a flash and the single, relatively slow shutter speed might hinder your plans, especially if your subject has the ability to move. But where some see limitation, others see artistic possibility. To this day enthusiasts enjoy creating, documenting, and experimenting with cameras just like this one.

CUSTOMER SATISFACTION: Taking photos is easy, the challenge is getting them developed.

SPY "PEN" RADIO

SPY "PEN" RADIO

Real Working Radio Hidden in Pen Case!

Fits Into Your Pocket Like Pen!

Hear SPORTS, MUSIC, LATEST NEWS AND EVENTS in office, school, bed, etc. Slips into pocket like ordinary pen. Tiny earphone for listening. Full range tuner. Guaranteed to pull in several stations in your area, although reception will vary from place to place. No additional expense. NO BATTERIES NEEDED. Self-powered solid state circuit. Germanium diode type radio (pulls in radio waves from air). Ground wire included but not always necessary in most areas. Complete, ready-to-play. Money back if not delighted.

☐ 7052. Pen Radio $3.75

SPY "PEN" RADIO

Item # 7052
Johnson Smith Company
Mt. Clemens, Mich. 48043

☆ No Batteries, Electricity
☆ Ready to Operate
☆ Nothing to Wear Out

Fits Into Your Pocket!

Working Radio Concealed In Pen Case

FACTS ABOUT YOUR SPY PEN RADIO: Your new radio is actually a germanium diode radio. It receives its power from the radio broadcasting stations in your area. The frequency waves broadcasted by the stations flow through the air and are "induced" into the metal structures and wires in or near your home. Then the germanium and internal ferrite loop rectify and tune this signal energy. This rectified energy is amplified by your earphone permitting your private listening pleasure. **PEN RADIO RECEPTION:** Best reception is obtained when there are no high voltage lines nearby. You may also discover that you will get better reception in one building than in another. If you do not get reception immediately, try another location or wait until later in the day. If you live in the country with no nearby broadcasting stations, clip the antenna to a plain piece of wire strung between trees or to a metal object that is outdoors. Reception in rural areas may also improve at night. Your "Pen Radio" will often work in some areas without attaching the clip to any grounded metal, but if you are near any grounded metal parts, follow the instructions in # 1 below.

HOW TO OPERATE THE PEN RADIO

1. Connect your contact clip to any one of the many grounded metal parts in your home. For example: the metal on the telephone dial, TV antenna, metal handle of a water faucet, radiator valve, drain pipes, wire fence, etc.

2. Put ear plug in ear.

3. The pen point is the tuning rod of the radio. Simply slide it in and out very slowly to tune into your radio station.

WE IMAGINED: A working radio concealed in a pen, opening up a world of covert radio-listening opportunities.

THEY SENT: An actual working radio concealed in the casing of a pen. Spies might be troubled by the two not-so-hidden, protruding wires connecting the earpiece and the grounding clamp, respectively. Secrecy is problematic when you've got a wire running to your ear and another tethered to a metal object. But concerns over stealthiness are quickly overshadowed by the radio's coolness.

It's tiny, especially for its time, and as advertised, it requires no batteries. Fine-tuning is cleverly achieved by adjusting the length of the antenna. Link it to grounded metal (though recommended sources like radiators and TV antennas are scarce these days), and you can instantly enjoy all that AM radio has to offer.

CUSTOMER SATISFACTION: So fun you won't mind if people see you using it.

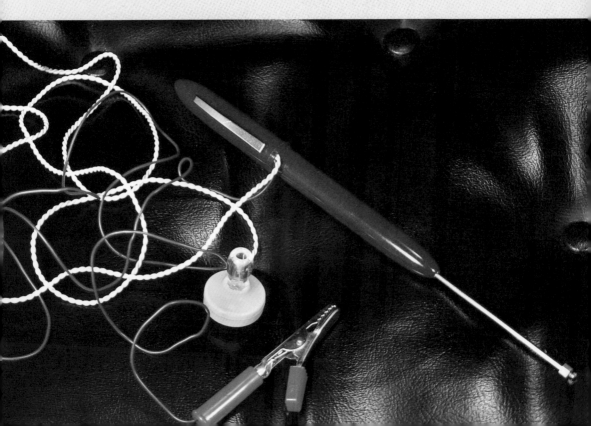

BUILD A WORKING LASER PISTOL

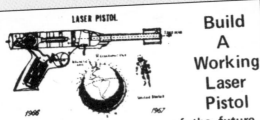

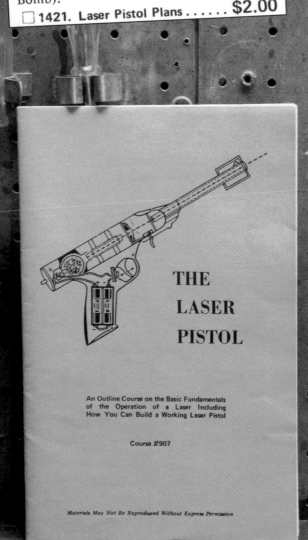

Build A Working Laser Pistol

Discover the power source of the future. Build your own operating Laser Pistol. If available commercially this portable Laser gun would cost well over $200. Easy to read drawings, instructions, explanations into the principles of Lasers with accompanying parts lists, names, addresses of manufacturers. Complete 16 page booklet used by Argonne National Laboratory (home of the Atomic Bomb).

☐ **1421. Laser Pistol Plans $2.00**

THE LASER PISTOL

An Outline Course on the Basic Fundamentals of the Operation of a Laser Including How You Can Build a Working Laser Pistol

Course #907

Materials May Not Be Reproduced Without Express Permission

WE IMAGINED: Schematics detailing construction of a sophisticated laser weapon, an essential device in every spy's arsenal—or in anyone's, really.

THEY SENT: A booklet outlining how to project a harmless light beam from a toy gun using items like wire, glue, copper tubing, a mirror, flash cubes, batteries, and a plastic lasing rod. The task appears challenging for even a devout *Popular Mechanics* subscriber, let alone a kid. The laser's inability to disintegrate is more of blow considering the ad's boast that it's "used by the Argonne National Laboratory (Home of the Atomic Bomb)."

CUSTOMER SATISFACTION: Zapped.

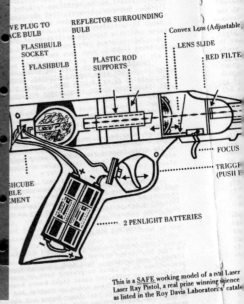

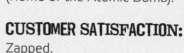

VE PLUG TO
CE BULB

REFLECTOR SURROUNDING
BULB

FLASHBULB
SOCKET

FLASHBULB

PLASTIC ROD
SUPPORTS

Convex Lens (Adjustable,

LENS SLIDE

RED FILTE

SHCUBE
BLE
MENT

2 PENLIGHT BATTERIES

FOCUS

TRIGGE
(PUSH B

This is a <u>SAFE</u> working model of a real Laser Laser Ray Pistol, a real prize winning science as listed in the Roy Davis Laboratori's catale

TRICKERY

Deception is a powerful tool and every young consumer had a choice: Do you fool others for their amusement or at their expense? When you consider that the pranks drastically outnumbered the magic tricks, it's pretty clear what most kids chose.

DISGUISES

FANGS
These plastic teeth (?) fit over your own teeth and, needless to say, they'll completely change your appearance—for the worse. We think they're too much, but why not let your friends be the judges?
Item No. 836   25c

WE IMAGINED: The means to alter our identity, whether to scare friends, blend in, entertain, or gain sympathy.

THEY SENT: Appliances that were good for some laughs yet rarely lived up to the realism we craved. These were mere toys and not the types of things that an international spy kept in his briefcase. Still, comic book mail-order provided a valuable service by offering year-round access to costumes. October came and went way too fast, and every kid knows that dressing up isn't just for Halloween.

CUSTOMER SATISFACTION: More "community theater" than "Hollywood."

WINKIN MONSTER EYE
Apply it to the forehead. P.S. It will stick and wink at the same time. No 121
EYEBALL CLOSES   75¢

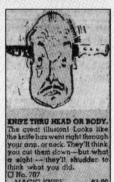

KNIFE THRU HEAD OR BODY.
The great illusion! Looks like the knife has went right through your arm, or neck. They'll think you cut them down—but what a sight—they'll shudder to think what you did.
☐ No. 207
MAGIC KNIFE $1.00

PHONY CAST
Imitation white plaster arm cast complete with arm sling. Looks like the real thing! Fits teenagers or adults.
A 4 $1.50

SCARFACE
A plastic scar that looks so realistic. Put one in the face and get lots of sympathy and pity.
№ 111   50¢

A rubber black eye so natural looking that it will fool anyone. Nicely painted by hand with gauze and adhesive tape attached. Ready to use and can be attached quickly. Packed individually with instruction slip in a colorful box. $1.00

SKIN HEAD WIG
Most people try to grow hair. This is just the opposite. Made of flesh toned latex to fit all heads, really changes your appearance.
No. A36 $1.00

ARROW THRU HEAD #014
$2.00
SOME ITEMS RE

MYSTIC SMOKE

WE IMAGINED: A hidden pyrotechnic device that makes our hands appear to be burning.

THEY SENT: A tube of goo called Mystic Smoke that provides a surprisingly realistic illusion. A tiny amount of the gel-like compound is placed between the thumb and forefinger, and as they are repeatedly pulled apart, threadlike strands are emitted that effectively resemble smoke. There are two distinct disadvantages: It's tough to get off your fingers, and it smells a bit like burnt hair.

BEHIND THE MYSTERY: The formula for Mystic Smoke was accidentally discovered by a New Jersey chemist and sold exclusively to the S. S. Adams Company.

CUSTOMER SATISFACTION:
Mystic Smoke does the trick.

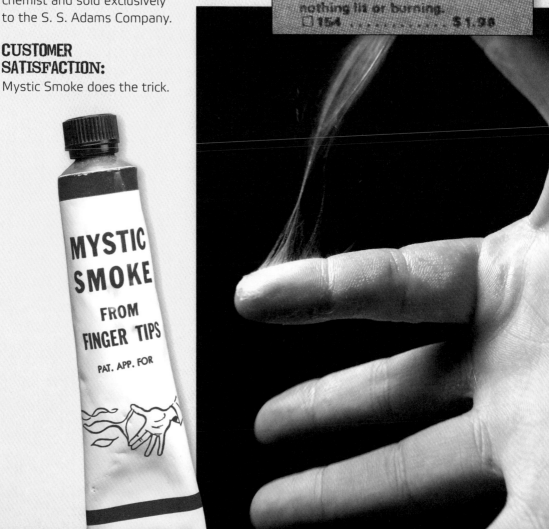

SMOKING FINGERS

SMOKE FROM YOUR FINGERS. Amaze and amuse your friends. After showing empty hands, reach out and produce clouds of actual smoke from your finger tips. Harmless . . . nothing lit or burning.
☐ 154 . . . . $1.98

MYSTIC SMOKE FROM FINGER TIPS

PAT. APP. FOR

SNEEZING POWDER

WE IMAGINED: The power to send a room into an uncontrollable sneezing fit.

THEY SENT: Finely ground pepper that is blown or projected into the face of a victim. It works, but the prankster must get dangerously close to administer the gag.

BEHIND THE MYSTERY: The earliest version of sneezing powder was a toxic chemical called dianisidine, which was banned by the FDA and has been utilized as a chemical weapon. Sneezing powder was also the very first of hundreds of gags designed by the prank pioneer S. S. Adams Company.

CUSTOMER SATISFACTION: Instant nasal spray.

SNEEZING POWDER. Place a little of this powder on your hand, blow into the air, step back and watch the fun begin. Everyone in the room will begin to sneeze without knowing why. More fun than a barrel full of monkeys.
☐ **No. 104**   **25¢ Each**
          5 for $1.00

HARMLESS FUN!
To make your victim sneeze, simply blow some toward him, off the back of your hand. Or, sprinkle some on a table. When a magazine is tossed down, it will whirl powder into the air.

KER CHOO!

SNEEZE POWDER

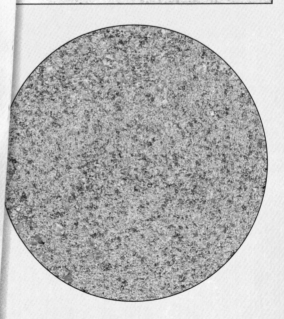

ABOVE: A close-up of Sneezing Powder.

ITCHING POWDER

WE IMAGINED: A way to really irritate your friends and enemies.

THEY SENT: Ground up organic irritants such as rose hip, the fruit of a rose plant. Bare flesh is no match for it.

CUSTOMER SATISFACTION: Powerful powder.

ITCHING POWDER. The more they scratch the more they itch. But it down their neck, in their . that's all you need em scratching like rt your own itching DAY. large Package $1.25

JUCK PULVER

Itching-Powder
Poil à gratter · Polvere da grattare
Polvo para esconzor
Jeukpoeder

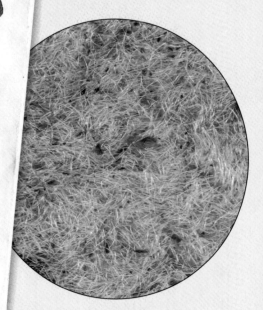

ABOVE: A close-up of Itching Powder.

NOVELTY HALL OF FAME

FUZZ-Y PUSS GLASSES. This is the well known instant disguise that's good for a million laughs. The horn-rimmed glasses have a big nose, bushy eyebrows and mustache attached. One of the greatest gag items ever.
#BP-446 . . . . $1.98

WHOOPEE CUSHION
Place it on a chair under a cushion, then watch the fun when someone sits down! It gives forth embarrassing noises. Made of rubber, and inflatable. A scream at parties and gatherings.
No. 247 . . . . **50c**

JOY BUZZER
Windup novelty you wear like a ring. Your victim gets a "SHOCKING" hand shake. Absolutely harmless.
No. 239   Only 50c

TALKING TEETH
They walk, talk, clickety-clack and yackety-yak.
#255 $1.75

"FAKE CHICKEN"
#001
$5.95

WE IMAGINED: The tools necessary to achieving laughs, "life of the party" status, and sweet, sweet attention.

THEY SENT: Novelty items that have transcended the dime stores to become bona fide cultural icons representing the very essence of humor. This elite breed of novelties includes the following members:

The Beagle Puss by Franco-American Novelty was inspired by Groucho Marx and supposedly designed by the brother of Louis St. Pierre, the proprietor of the Hollywood Magic Shop.

The Whoopee Cushion is from the JEM Rubber Company. Conceived by the employees of JEM and sold to the Johnson Smith Company, but only after the S. S. Adams Company passed on the product on the grounds of "poor taste." Once it was a proven success, Adams made the similar Razzberry Cushion.

The Super Joy Buzzer, from the S. S. Adams Company, was developed by the king of pranks himself, Samuel Sorenson Adams, with help from a Jewish craftsman living in Nazi Germany.

Talking Teeth, made by H. Fishlove and Company, was created by legendary toy and game inventor Eddie Goldfarb for Marvin Glass and Associates. They were said to be inspired by Goldfarb's mother-in-law.

The Rubber Chicken is from the Loftus Novelty Company. Its origins are unsubstantiated, though one theory is that it was first produced by Loftus, possibly based on the act of the influential nineteenth-century British clown Joseph Grimaldi.

CUSTOMER SATISFACTION: Critics say they're no longer funny. Ten-year-olds disagree.

BULLET HOLES

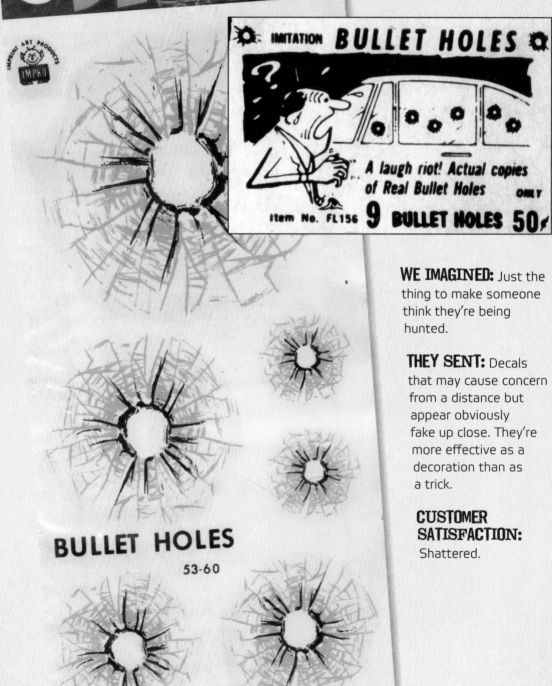

WE IMAGINED: Just the thing to make someone think they're being hunted.

THEY SENT: Decals that may cause concern from a distance but appear obviously fake up close. They're more effective as a decoration than as a trick.

CUSTOMER SATISFACTION: Shattered.

EXHAUST WHISTLE

WE IMAGINED: A way to humble those lucky people who are old enough to drive.

THEY SENT: A funny-looking piece of metal that really does create a ruckus when you attach it to a tailpipe. Just hope your victim doesn't have an accident.

CUSTOMER SATISFACTION:
A real scream.

PRANKSTER WHISTLE

Greatest gag in years. Just place inside any tail-pipe and watch the fun. As soon as he starts the car it will sound as if the whole motor fell out. It's a panic, but completely harmless.

No. F-22 . . . . only 75c

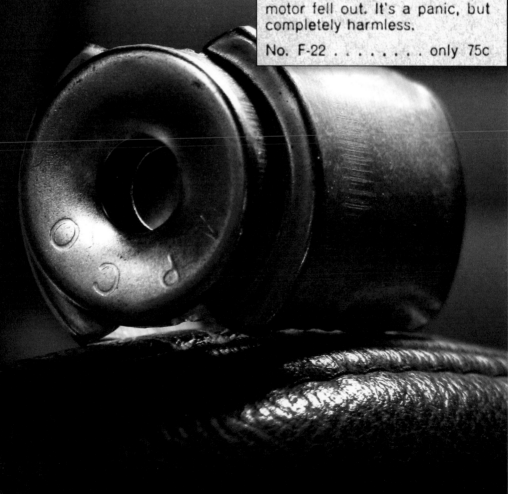

TABLE GAGS

WE IMAGINED:
An assortment of instruments capable of transforming any meal into a madcap event worthy of a Three Stooges film.

THEY SENT: Us to our room. Dinnertime is prime time for a budding prankster. It's when both victim and audience assemble in one place. The gag-master faces as many decisions as the host of the meal. How subtle or disruptive should the prank be? A quivering plate can be amusing, while instant worms might merit a scream. How smart is the rube? Do they know that peanuts aren't sold in tin cans? How reliable is the joke itself? Some bug-infested ice cubes don't even float!

CUSTOMER SATISFACTION: Feast or famine, depending on the prankster.

HOT SEAT. Funniest gag ever! It's like a miniature electric chair. Just place it on your favorite victim's seat or in his pocket. In a few seconds he will hit the ceiling as it becomes sizzling hot.
□ No. 102   35¢ Each
                   3 for $1.00

A list th... send for foreign s... showtick... ers, etc. the askin... worth of No. F-12... 3 lists .

FLY IN ICE
Scare your friends! Just drop this life-like ice cube with a fly inside it into someone's drink and watch his eyes pop–ugh.

No. F-16 . . . . only 50c

□ 1058. Playboy Decals $1.1...

Foaming Sugar Only 39¢
Add a teaspoon to victim's favorite bevera... and the fun begins. Flows over the top lik... volcano. □ 2157. . . . . 1...

975 Catalog

WORMS
Drop these seemingly innocent pellets into a glass of water and magically a worm will appear. Can you imagine the look of horror on your victims face? It's harmless.

$2.95 SNAKE NUT CAN

Offer to friends or leave on table or counter, stand back & watch the fun. Somebody is sure to want to help themselves sooner or later. Looks like real can of mixed nuts but is loaded with cloth-covered 30" spring "snake" that shoots out. Works on even most suspicious victims.
2927. Snake Nut Can. $2.95

WHOOPS
Looks like someone lost their lunch. Place it on the floor and wait for your first unsuspecting victim to walk in—ugh. Better catch him before he faints. No. 9016 . . . . Only .75

Phony Squirt Catsup
Plastic containers look like they should hold the real thing. So when you "squirt" at friends or relatives they'll think their clothes are ruined. Red or yellow string shoots out causing big commotion. Every prankster should have both of these in his arsenal for special occasions.
□ 2639. Phony Catsup $2.15
□ 2720. Phony Mustard $2.15

PLATE LIFTER
Plate lifter consists of a long rubber hose with a lifter on one end and a bulb on the other. Use it under a plate to spill the soup or under vest to imitate heart beat, or under bedclothes as a mouse, etc.
No. 2164. . . . . 50¢

SNOWSTORM TABLETS

SNOWSTORM TABLETS. Make it snow anytime of the year indoors. Fill a whole room with "snow". Just place one of these almost invisible tablets on the end of a cigarette and watch them run for their sleds. Several storms to a package. No. 155 . . . 2 packages $1.25

CIGARETTE SNOW STORM

BRRRR

NIEVE ARTIFICIAL
One tablet placed on a glowing cigarette or cigar makes a terrific indoor snow storm.
Do not swallow; injurious to heal h, if misused (contents of bag 0,5 g metaidehyde).
MADE IN W. GERMANY

WE IMAGINED: An explosive device that produces a cloud of ash.

THEY SENT: A packet of a dozen pill-like tablets. When applied to the ember of a cigarette, each tablet froths with fuzzy clusters of lighter-than-air fibers that float about the room, although the output is exaggerated in the ad. There's no explosion, but they make up for it with a chemical stench that makes you wonder if they're more harmful than cigarettes.

CUSTOMER SATISFACTION:
Works, but may need a Surgeon General's warning.

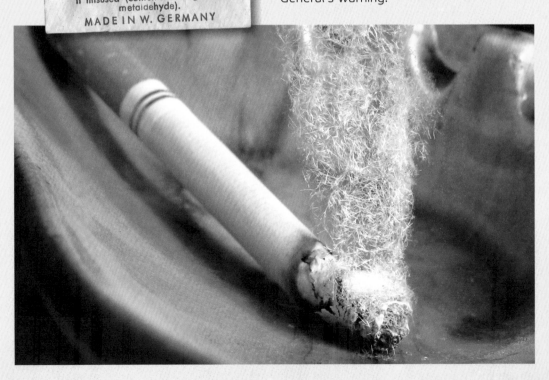

7-11 MAGIC DICE

7-11 MAGIC DICE
Set includes 2 pairs of dice—one regular and one that only rolls sevens or elevens.
#088 $2.00

WE IMAGINED: A pair of secretly weighted dice that always land on seven or eleven.

THEY SENT: Two sets of dice; one pair is normal, and the other pair is made up of one die with fives on every side and another bearing only twos and sixes. Thus, rolling seven or eleven is guaranteed, but deception is virtually impossible: Should you possess the slight-of-hand skills to alternate between the real and fake dice without notice, you'd still need to keep your opponent from actually looking at the dice after you roll. Not the sort of thing you'd want to try at a casino or in a street corner game of craps. Lastly, these are half the size of standard dice. Of course they are.

CUSTOMER SATISFACTION:
Crapped out.

MAGIC DISCS

MAGIC DISCS
When you know the secret of Magic Discs they will amaze and thrill you & your friends. Place disc on flat surface and watch it take off! It JUMPS up to 5 feet. Instructions & games list included No. 110   2 for $1.00

WE IMAGINED: Hmmm, a gray oval? There's no telling . . .

THEY SENT: A metallic silver disc, about the size of a quarter. The "secret" is that the disc is slightly concave. When it's pushed in and placed on a table, it stays dormant momentarily before jumping upward as it pops back into shape.

CUSTOMER SATISFACTION: Little circle, big suspense.

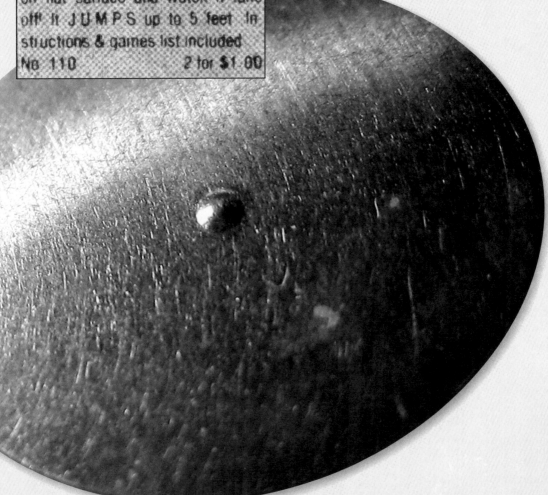

ABOVE: Magic Disc shown 525 percent larger than actual size.

FLASHING EYES

FLASHING EYES. Used by many magicians! By simply blinking your eyes open and shut, they appear as streaks of lightning. Brilliant sparks seem to flash out of your eyes. The more you blink, the more sparks and flashes seem to fly out. Easy to do. No wires! No chemicals! Absolutely safe. A beautiful effect. Very astonishing!

No . S6   50¢

WE IMAGINED: A revolutionary device that emits sparks and even lightning from your eyes.

THEY SENT: Xeroxed instructions on how to put pieces of tin foil on your eyelids.

CUSTOMER SATISFACTION: Foiled again!

Flashing Eyes
****

A Startling & Novel Effect for Any Show

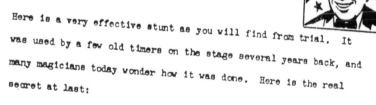

Here is a very effective stunt as you will find from trial. It was used by a few old timers on the stage several years back, and many magicians today wonder how it was done. Here is the real secret at last:

Obtain some silver paper and cut out two small triangles, like tiny slices of pie. Stick one to each eye lid at the top, the pointed end down. When the eyes are open they are not seen. Now, by blinking the eyes with a spotlight or footlight shining on your face, they appear as streaks of lightning or sparks shooting from the eyes. The more you blink the more sparks seem to fly from the eyes. The illusion at a short distance is really GREAT. Little things like this often create more mystery and talk than some great tricks.

You will find that the tin foil from a cigarette package works fine for this effect.

MAGIC TRICKS

WE IMAGINED: The ability to dazzle and astonish for fun and profit and to emulate the classiest people of all—magicians.

THEY SENT: An assortment of odd-looking doodads that seem maddeningly simplistic once you learn the secret operating procedures.

BEHIND THE MYSTERY: Over time, elaborate and once-perplexing stage illusions have devolved into these crude plastic gimmicks. However, the principles behind them are strong enough to continue to mystify generation after generation of young audiences. Buyers of these tricks are taking part in a rich tradition that's centuries old and laden with secrecy. The most successful modern-day illusionists almost universally testify that their interest in the art was spawned because of dime-store effects such as these.

CUSTOMER SATISFACTION: Amazing.

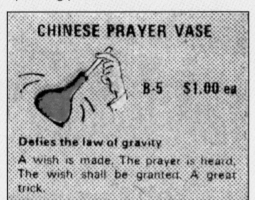

CHINESE PRAYER VASE

B-5 $1.00 ea

Defies the law of gravity.

A wish is made. The prayer is heard. The wish shall be granted. A great trick.

Floats In Mid-Air Without Support

KING TUT MUMMY

MYSTERY MUMMY COMES TO LIFE! Amazing, miraculous. No skill required. Floats in air or lies down at your will. Lasts indefinitely. Wonderful pocket mystery.

☐ 3263. Mummy .... 95¢

MYSTERY LIGHT BULB

This bulb, when held in hand, lights whenever desired. A spectator can NOT make it light unless he knows the secret.

#143 $2.²⁵

29¢

Live Action Miracle Mouse

Runs, climbs, crawls at your command. Acts almost like real thing. Make it do amazing tricks. Jumps from hand to hand. Climbs up glass, sleeve, out of hat, etc. Fool your friends. No motor. No rubber bands.

☐ 3401. Miracle Mouse.............29¢

CIGARETTE CATCHER

G-14   .50¢ ea

Cigarettes in a never ending stream, may be plucked from the air, and dropped in a hat. The hand is quicker than the eye.

MAGIC FINGER CHOPPER

Two cigarettes are inserted in holes and are chopped in half by slashing knife blade. THEN—insert your finger (to show you possess secret powers) or "borrow" your friend's finger (they're not sure if they're going to get it back!) Everything turns out all right—bottom cigarette is slashed but not the finger. Why? Sensational! Attractive apparatus. Complete.

No. 3176. $1.00
Postpaid......

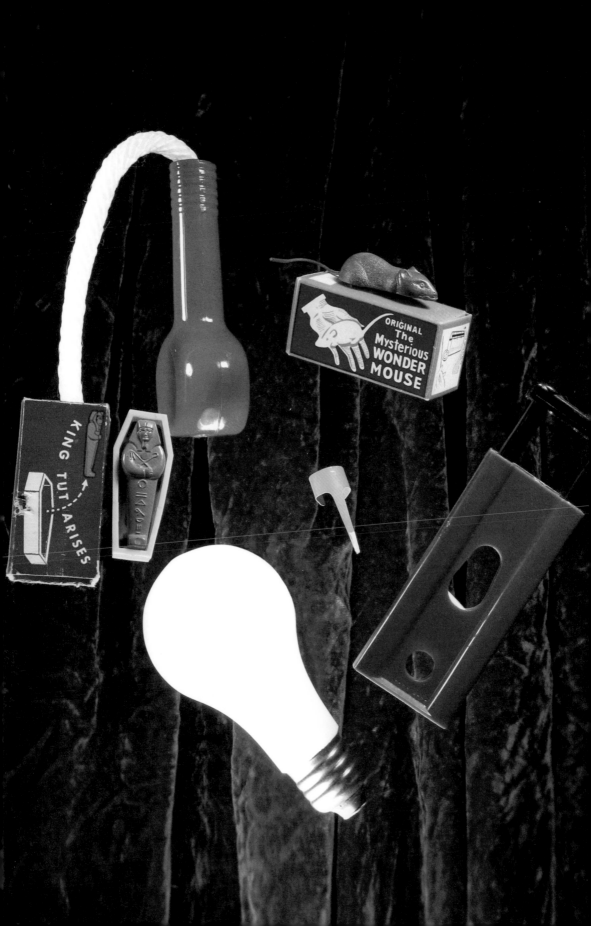

ODDITIES

If you wish to experience that which is bizarre and puzzling, you needn't book an expensive safari nor consult Robert L. Ripley. An unexplained world lurks within the deepest pages of yesteryear's comic magazines. There you will unearth a treacherous terrain of misfit concepts and glorious misfires.

SEA-MONKEYS

WE IMAGINED: New pets that look like happy, naked, aquatic families capable of performing tricks and stunts and playing games.

THEY SENT: Dormant embryos of brine shrimp in a state of suspended animation that hatch when exposed to purified water. In their earliest stages the tiny white sea creatures are almost indistinguishable from other floating debris, but their movement becomes apparent with help from the included magnifying glass. As the weeks pass, no faces appear, but the shrimp do develop tiny dark eyes, which is all most owners need to establish a deep personal connection with the little guys.

BEHIND THE MYSTERY: Like X-Ray Spex, Sea-Monkeys were marketed by Harold von Braunhut. Initially, retail buyers weren't interested in them, which forced Braunhut to reach the public directly by way of comic book ads. The relatively affordable ad space proved to be a tremendous success, and Harold's "Instant Life" produced instant wealth. In their prime, Sea-Monkeys ads appeared in 303 million pages annually.

CUSTOMER SATISFACTION: From heartbreaking to heartwarming.

LEFT: A close-up of a real Sea-Monkey.

ABOVE: The first Sea-Monkey artwork was provided by world record–holding high diver Henri LaMothe. Subsequent ad art was drawn by the former vice president of DC Comics, Joe Orlando.

SMOKING PET

SMOKING PETS Ever see a pet smoke? Well, this one does. Just insert a special "cigaret" into his mouth . . . light up and watch him smoke away. Even blows smoke rings! Truly amazing effect. Special - Two Smokie Pets & Extra Cigarettes **89¢**

Order No. SP379

WE IMAGINED: Either cigarettes for animals or a toy that can smoke.

THEY SENT: A plastic dog that holds mini, pseudo cigarettes in its mouth. A variety of smoking characters were also available, including monkeys, cats, mules, and babies. The smoke is not an illusion. Real fire is involved, which is one of a multitude of taboos that were shattered by these playthings. The simulated "cigarettes" themselves emit tiny bursts of smoke in short intervals; they even form smoke rings sometimes. The pets are just a decoration, so once you have the fake cigarettes, you can give any toy an apparent nicotine habit.

CUSTOMER SATISFACTION: Up in smoke.

LIFE-LIKE LADY'S LEGS

Life-Like Lady's Legs

So realistic, they fool everyone. Creates laugh riot when poking out from embarrassing places. Carry in pocket. Use over & over. Inflatable vinyl. About 36" long.

☐ 3918. Life-Like Legs
$3.95

WE IMAGINED: Legs so realistic they'll fool anyone.

THEY SENT: Inflatable legs that aren't at all realistic. In addition to unsightly seams, and a bright pink hue, they don't come with shoes. Sure, you could go to the trouble of buying high heels and pantyhose, but then the joke's on you.

CUSTOMER SATISFACTION: Unladylike.

VERY SPECIAL PEOPLE

WE IMAGINED: An insightful, compassionate, and dignified look at people who were born different. We're glad it's "not just a picture book of freaks," as the ad says, because we'd never want something like that. No, sir.

THEY SENT: A 400-page book that features 27 pages of black-and-white photos and 380 pages of text that was likely ignored. The stories are tasteful and touching, but most young readers were just looking for a freak show. The publication cost a pretty penny by kiddie mail-order standards; it was $6.95 in 1975, which could have paid for nearly sixteen gallons of gas.

BEHIND THE MYSTERY: Frederick Drimmer (1916–2000) is the author of *The Elephant Man, Until You Are Dead* (a history of executions in the United States), and *Scalps and Tomahawks*, a book of Native American captivities.

CUSTOMER SATISFACTION: Stimulating, until you matured enough to feel guilty for seeking this type of entertainment.

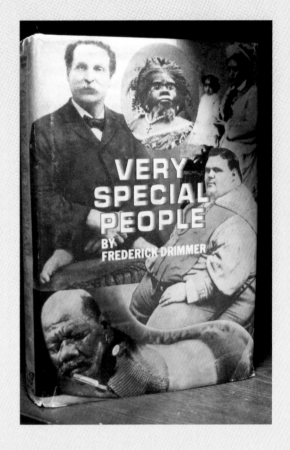

"NOBODY LOVES THE HULK"

WE IMAGINED: A song about the Hulk for one dollar.

THEY SENT: An unauthorized, slapdash song about the Hulk for one dollar.

BEHIND THE MYSTERY: "Nobody Loves the Hulk" is the handiwork of some recording artists calling themselves the Traits, who had no affiliation with the well-established group Roy Head and the Traits. Released in 1969, the single was an attempted cash-grab following the mega success of "Sugar Sugar" by the Archies, a fictitious pop music group based on the comic book characters. The fact that Queen City Records is misnamed Queens City on the label is just one indication of the time they invested in the project.

CUSTOMER SATISFACTION:
Hulk Smash!

VENUS FLY TRAP

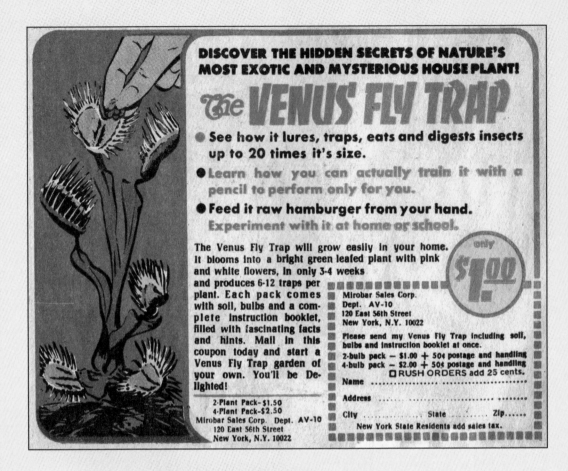

WE IMAGINED: An energetic, insect-eating pet that could possibly be trained to eat bullies.

THEY SENT: Soil and a pack of seeds that often stayed seeds forever. Green-thumbed kids wound up with the coolest plant in the world, even though it remained motionless and didn't crave mean kids.

CUSTOMER SATISFACTION: You reap what you sow.

LEFT: A pot of mail-order Venus Fly Trap seeds after four months of care.

TONGA BANANA STAMP

WE IMAGINED: A novel, foreign stamp.

THEY SENT: Stamps that were not only eye-appealing and irregularly shaped, they had self-adhesive backs so they required no licking! These days the selection of US stamps are as colorful and diverse as a sixth grader's sticker collection. It's easy to forget that not so long ago stamp designs were rife with stodgy presidential profiles. The Kingdom of Tonga was a postal pioneer.

CUSTOMER SATISFACTION: Stamp of approval.

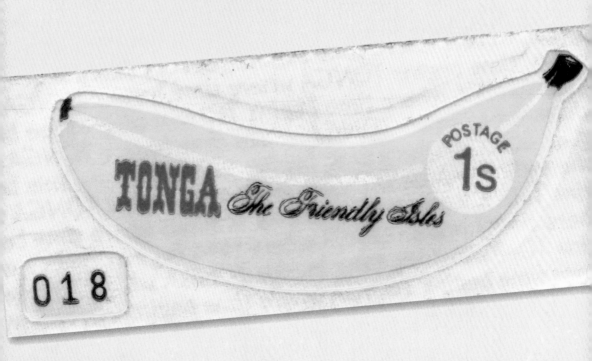

TRICK BASEBALL

WE IMAGINED: A baseball that is somehow weighted or even remote controlled to achieve effects popularized by Bugs Bunny.

THEY SENT: Three-quarters of a molded rubber baseball that was designed to give any pitcher the ability to throw a curveball. The instructions include detailed procedures on how to throw curveballs, screwballs, sinkers, and risers depending on where you hold the flat side and where you aim. On the playing field the effect is probably more evident, but when tested in a backyard game of catch, the missing slab didn't seem to alter the ball's flight.

BEHIND THE MYSTERY: "Major League Breaking Balls," as they are officially called, were actually used in Major League training at one time. The novelty was originated by former minor league pitcher Nelson Newcomb and his son Corky.

CUSTOMER SATISFACTION: Foul ball.

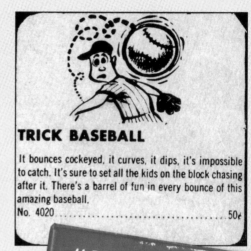

TRICK BASEBALL

It bounces cockeyed, it curves, it dips, it's impossible to catch. It's sure to set all the kids on the block chasing after it. There's a barrel of fun in every bounce of this amazing baseball.
No. 4020 .... 50¢

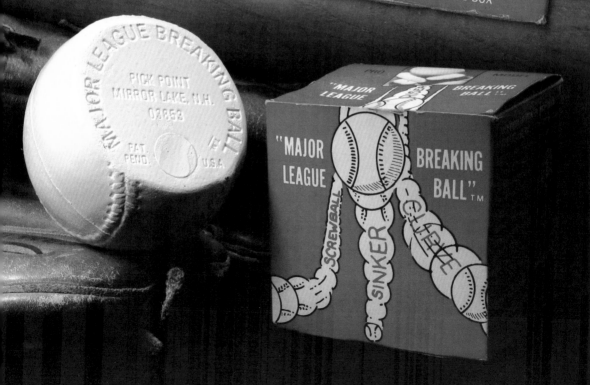

"MAJOR LEAGUE BREAKING BALL" T.M.

THE BASEBALL THAT <u>ANYONE</u> CAN CURVE SO HITTERS CAN HIT UNLIMITED CURVES, SINKERS, SCREWBALLS AND RISERS!

★ OFFICIAL WEIGHT & SIZE ★

INSTRUCTIONS INSIDE BOX

MYSTERY ELECTRONIC TOP

WE IMAGINED: A top that mysteriously spins for days.

THEY SENT: A dinky little top that's scantly taller than a thimble and a massive base that is required to achieve super spinning power. The "brain busting" energy source is a nine-volt battery that powers a conductive coil in the base. When the top crosses the center of the base, the coil activates and speeds up the "radially oriented magnetic field," causing it to spin faster. Since the top is only in the center when it slows down, the life of the battery is prolonged.

CUSTOMER SATISFACTION:
Goes from dizzying to fascinating.

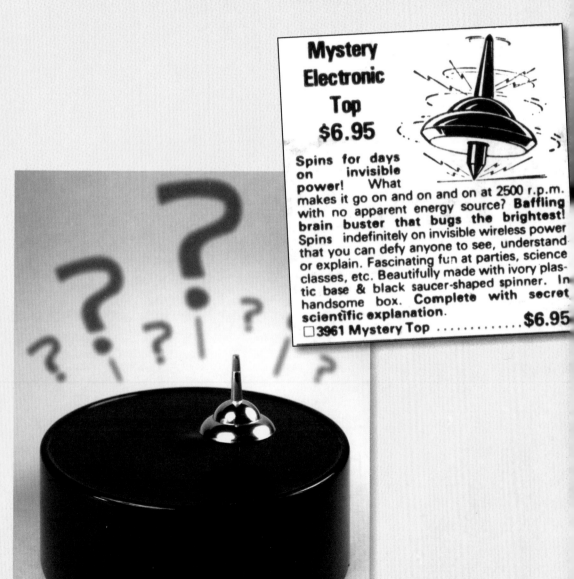

BAG FULL OF LAUGHS

WE IMAGINED: A mysterious bag that somehow laughs.

THEY SENT: A fabric bag that conceals a plastic box containing a low-tech, battery-operated record player. When the plunger is pressed, a motor turns a rubber band that spins a recording of some highly disturbing laughter.

Electric Laughing Bag

Roars with Laughter! Happy, hilarious joke, gift or surprise. Battery operated. Lasts indefinitely.

3070 .. $3.95

BEHIND THE MYSTERY: While other toy companies were using similar portable playback devices in dolls and stuffed animals, J. Swedlin Inc. preferred to stick them inside inanimate objects, mostly bags. They trademarked over a dozen, including the Cry'n Bag, Nifty Thrifty money bag bank, Just "Fore" Laughs golf bag, Bag of Bull, Doggy Bag, Gab Bag, and Fun in a Sack. The technology came at a price. In 1974 the silly sacks cost nearly four dollars.

CUSTOMER SATISFACTION:
Not enough yuks for the bucks.

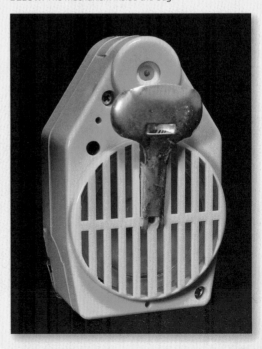

BELOW: The mechanism inside the bag.

CHICK INCUBATOR

WE IMAGINED: Hatching our own pets; an endless supply of eggs.

THEY SENT: Four real fertile eggs and a plastic chamber for hatching live chicken eggs that's heated with a Christmas light.

BEHIND THE MYSTERY: GQF Manufacturing have been making their own incubators since the 1960s, and their professional units are met with much praise. The more affordable Chick-bator is made for kids, particularly budding farmers. A common criticism is that it doesn't heat well enough to hatch the eggs, but perhaps that's a good thing. After "the miracle of birth" is over, you're left with a quartet of birds that are a lot louder and messier than Sea-Monkeys.

CUSTOMER SATISFACTION:
You may be sorry if it works.

SURPRISE PACKAGE

Most distributors offered some version of the Surprise Package. These collections were commonly known to be a means of unloading discontinued product. Despite knowing that these were the least-wanted items in the entire inventory, customers couldn't escape the lure of a potential bargain. Perhaps even more enticing was the underlying mystery, and it was a riddle you could solve for only fifty cents.

101 MAGIC TRICKS. Anyone can do them! No skill or sleight-of-hand required! Do amazing tricks with cards, coins, paper, pencils, cigarettes, handkerchiefs, etc. One trick alone is worth the price of the entire book.
☐ No. 170   75¢

STINK LOADS. Push the load out of sight into a cigarette. After the first puff, it will taste awful and smell worse. Guaranteed to stop cigarette moochers.
☐ No. 814   2 Pkgs. $1.00

SNAPPERS Drop for E·X·T·R·A Loud explosion. #223   **$1.50**

#751 **$2.25**

PENNY INSIDE GLASS JUG
Mystery Lucky Pocket Charm. How did it get inside? Fully formed miniature glass jug, 1¼-in. high.
No. 8992.
Price, Postpaid. **50¢**

DISAPPEARING INK SQUIRTER #508 **$1.00**

FAKE DOGGIE DOO

LOUD NOSE BLOWER
Get roars of laughter -- insert this 'nose blower' in your handkerchief and blow. It sounds like the roof caved in! Really a riot!
No. F-23 . . . only 25¢

Squirt Jackpot Machine
Jackpot Of Laffs! 5" authentic replica of Las Vegas slot machine gives victim unsuspected "pay off"! In fact, anyone who pulls lever really "takes a bath." Wheels spin like real thing but funny little man pops up and shoots water right at player. Use over & over Fools everyone. Impossible to detect. Can also be played like realistic jackpot game. Odds shown on front. Sturdy plastic. Bright colors. Send $2.95 each. Add 75¢ shipping & handling.

Johnson Smith Company
Dept. 313, Mt. Clemens, Mich 48043

HOT PEPPER GUM. Flavored with delicious mint but hidden within the mint is RED HOT PEPPER! The more the chew the hotter it gets. Not harmful but a joke they'll remember. Package of 5 sticks.
☐ No. 174   2 pkgs. $1.00

SNAKE CIGARET LIGHTER
Looks like real thing. But when they try for a light, they get a real fright when snake shoots out right under their nose. Polished steel case.   **50¢**

Magnetic 'Live' PUPS
Magnetic fun-Loving Scotty Dogs are nation wide sensation. Put one Scotty behind the other and watch them spin. They twist, move, kiss in a fascinating, amusing manner, motivated by powerful Alnico magnets. No. motor, no springs. These powerful magnets make them perform many stunts. No. 2025. Postpaid............ 25¢

MAGIC SOAP POWDER. Sprinkle a little of this almost invisible magic powder on any soap. When anyone uses the soap their hands and face will turn bloody red. Have fun! Drives them crazy! Harmless!
☐ No. 123   30¢ pkg.
4 pkgs $1.00

SQUIRT CAMERA 69¢

They say "cheese" & you take picture they won't forget! You'd better be a fast runner!
☐ 2084. Squirt Camera ....69¢

Deluxe Electric Shock Pen—$9.95
When they borrow your expensive looking ball point pen it causes the sparks to fly. They push the button and THEY GET ZAPPED! The looks and feel of finest pen on market. Wear in pocket or leave on desk, ready for your next "victim." Never fails. Teaches "snitchers" a lesson. Expertly made by West German craftsmen. Deluxe in looks & results. With replaceable battery inside.

MAD MONSTER

MAD MONSTER IN PERFUME BOX - A SPIDER TUMBLES OUT OF HANDSOME PERFUME BOX.

ONLY $1.45

Crazy Action Billiard Balls   **$3.95**
Great way to break up a serious game of pool. Looks like regular ball until your unsuspecting victim hits it. Wanders erratically all over table with strangest "English" you've ever seen. Causes red faces & laugh riot. 2¼" regulation size.
☐ 2961. Crazy Cue Ball **$3.95**
☐ 2967. Crazy 8 Ball **$3.95**

EVERLITE CANDLES
Cannot be blown out. Great Gag!
#705   **$1.50**

Scary Skull
Looks ugly. For bike, car, cycle, etc. With hair. Synthetically made, but realistic looking. Often seen in carnivals and side-shows.
☐ 3742. Scary Skull .... 95¢

Rubber Dollars 59¢
Stretch your money. Printed on latex rubber to resemble currency. 3 per set.
☐ 2393. Rubber Bucks 59¢

AFTERWORD

GROWING UP is in large part about adjusting to a narrowing of possibility. With each year, we surrender what could have been. When you're seven, you can become a spaceman as easily as you can become a doctor. When you're a liberal arts major, you're still holding the door open for the possibility you might become a novelist. When you have children, your field of choices has slimmed to private sector structural engineer (good pay) or public sector structural engineer (good benefits).

Time speeds up, too. They say a fly can avoid your swat because it perceives time more slowly. A baseball game at twelve seems like a never-ending idyll. At forty, life can feel like a series of waves, crashing one after another across your back.

And what about knowledge? Gaining knowledge is wonderful. I'm thirty now, and I can change a tire, throw a spiral, do some basic functions in Excel. I couldn't do any of those things at seven. At seven, though, what I didn't know was just as wonderful as what I did. I remember opening the *Baseball Encyclopedia* just to look at names and numbers. Being as

close as I was to learning things like pants-buttoning and walking without falling, every shred of information seemed pregnant with the potential to explode into something fantastic. I could look at the name Van Lingle Mungo and instantly build a world around it. Or a dozen worlds, all living at once.

I remember being afraid as a kid. When my mom went to work or my dad to a meeting, I had to fill my mind with something because the sheer possibilities surrounding me were overwhelming. As much as it is liberating to have the world stretch out before you, it's terrifying as well. How will you manage? Every time you pick something, you're letting something else go.

I miss that overwhelming potential though. I've got all the power and control in the world—a wife, a car, a house, a stereo, books, collections, kitchen appliances—and yet I find myself wishing I had none.

The resonance of the cardboard trinkets in these pages comes from that sense of possibility. They promise us a chance to play in that possibility and to conquer the fear that comes with its immensity. The comic book is

a direct expression of possibility. What if the fears in our lives became powers? And what if the powers we read about in a comic book could be made real? In four to six weeks?

Some of these powers are straight from the pages of a comic. We're conquering our weakness, just like Charles Atlas did. Conquering our fear of the unknown—particularly the lady part of the unknown—with X-Ray Spex. Even more likely, they're about socialization. Hypnotism or magic tricks. Things that promise to make the change from child to adult smooth, to iron out the kinks. Take the Raquel Welch Pillow: the excitement of sexuality, merged with the familiar comfort of sleep.

I mail-order things all the time. I've become inured to the wait. It's like a double purchase for me now. One thrill from clicking "Buy," one from opening a package. When I was a kid, though, those four to six liminal weeks, the ones between buy and get, were interminable. They were the journey of possibility, the time when I actually allowed myself to believe that what I bought was what I hoped it might be.

Of course, the junk we got in the mail is junk, powerful only as metaphor. We all have to grow up, and we all do. We find our own ways to ask a girl to the prom or choose a career. We get stronger and tougher, inevitably. Some of the challenges, even when overcome, disappoint. Only a few of us grow up to be spacemen. And, of course, with each choice we make and each hill we climb, we lose a little bit of that possibility.

Now, though, we live in the age of eBay. If we want something, we can buy it, and so we do. Kirk Demarais has bought all the trinkets and built us a museum of promise and disappointment. Why are we drawn back to that world, again and again? Whatever power we may have as adults—changing tires, making new life—will never match the horizon that was before us as children. It's tragic, really, a little scar. Maybe, though, if we poke that scar a bit once in a while, we can remember that feeling when we were kids. When anything could happen, and we could have Powers.

—Jesse Thorn

APPENDIX

A sampler of full-page comic book ads from the 1960s and '70s.

Catalog covers from Honor House, Johnson Smith, and Fun Factory.

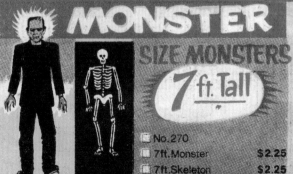

ACKNOWLEDGMENTS

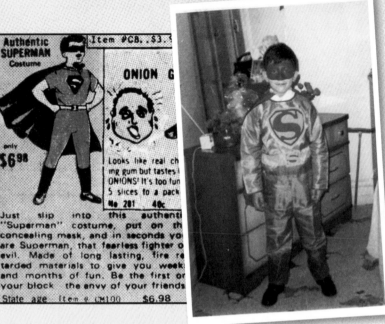

LEFT AND ABOVE: Eddie Guevara at age 11 wearing a Superman costume, purchased from an Honor House ad, and present-day Eddie.

I am exceedingly grateful to EDDIE GUEVARA, who was one of the lucky kids that managed to actually patronize the comic book novelty dealers. He wasn't let down by the primitive sketches that came when he ordered the plans to "build your own monster robot," instead he ordered another copy. As a young man, Eddie sought out every tidbit of available information related to comic book mail-order with the hopes of running his own novelty dealership. He visited post office boxes, tracked down former CEOs, and filled cabinets with fruitless paper trails to fly-by-night distributors. Eddie put his knowledge to the test in the late 1980s, when he started placing his own ads and then opened his own magic shop.

In 1992 he convinced the former Fun Factory owner to reopen for business by launching a brand new ad in DC Comics. Eddie achieved his dream; he revived a classic novelty house and found himself opening envelopes full of loose change and sending fun-makers to kids. Today he continues to offer classic mail-order items on his website HouseoftheUnusual.com.

Eddie's ability to save his childhood novelties and track down the ones that got away is the reason this book is so comprehensive. I consulted Eddie as soon as this project got underway. He generously opened up his collection and his home to me for the sake of this book, providing many of the rarest items featured.

I WOULD ALSO LIKE TO THANK

Mom
Chris Adams
George Atamian
Jason Babler
Harry Borgman
Jeff Campbell
Linn Carlson
Ray Castile
Jonathan Cobin
R. Darian
eBay
Brad Felts
Todd Franklin
Mark Frauenfelder
Barbara Genetin
Dan Goodsell

David Haversat
Jeffrey C. Hogue
Neal Holland
Jon Huckeby
Scott Kinney
Chip Kidd
Todd Knowlton
Chrissy Kwasnik
Cynthia Soroka
Devlin Thompson
Jesse Thorn
Yolanda von Braunhut
David Wahl
Mark Waid
Tim Walsh
Jason Willis

Special thanks to Kevin Toyama for endlessly championing this project.

Very special thanks to my dear wife and son. It's such a blessing getting to encounter life's mysteries with you.

COLOPHON

Publisher: Raoul Goff

Art Director: Jason Babler

Production Director: Anna Wan

Managing Editor: Kevin Toyama

Designer: Kirk Demarais

Photographer: Kirk Demarais

Copy Editor: Jeff Campbell

Production Editor: Jan Hughes

ADDITIONAL PHOTO CREDITS

Polaris Nuclear Sub photo courtesy of Clayton Moraga

Topstone Masks by Raymond Castile

Moon Monster by Mr. and Mrs. Jason Willis

Jet Rocket Spaceship boy from the collection of John Griffith and Angelica Paez of snapatorium.com

Jet Rocket Spaceship photo by R. Darian

"Artemia salina 1" by Hans Hillewaert used under Creative Commons Attribution-ShareAlike license

CONTRIBUTORS

100 Pirates, original sculpts, and footlocker artwork provided by Dan Goodsell

How To Draw Monsters provided by Harry Borgman

100 Toy Soldiers box provided by Todd Knowlton

Lagoon Monster Mask provided by Andy Williams

Charles Atlas imagery provided by Jeffrey C. Hogue and Scott Kinney

Blackhead remover, Mystic Smoke, and various ad scans provided by Todd Franklin of Neatocoolville.com

Various ads provided by Scott Kinney

Aqua-Spex, Hypno-Spex, Mini Pistol variant, Spud Gun variant, 6-Foot Monster Size Monsters, 7-Foot Monster Size Monsters, U-Control Ghost, Monster Ghost, Moon Monster variant, 7 Gigantic Dinosaurs, Monster Plans, Raquel Welch Pillow, Mini Skull Flashlight, 9-Foot Hot Air Balloon, Secret Book Safe, Secret Spy Scope, Laser Pistol Plans, Snowstorm Tablets, Honor House catalog, Skeleton model, Fun Factory coupons, and Flashing Eyes all courtesy of Eddie Guevara.

ABOUT THE AUTHOR

KIRK DEMARAIS

YOU IMAGINED: An agreeable gentleman who's really got his act together. Actually, you probably haven't given it much thought.

BEHIND THE MYSTERY: Kirk Demarais is a freelance creator and author of *Life of the Party*, a visual history of the S.S. Adams Prank and Magic Company.

He wrote and directed *Flip*, an award-winning short film inspired by mail-order novelties, and he codirected *Foot*, an animated film distributed by bobblehead maker FunKo.

In addition to neglecting his retro culture website, SecretFunSpot.com, Kirk's pop-surrealist artwork is regularly shown at L.A.'s Gallery 1988. Kirk enjoys life in the hills of Arkansas with his wife and son and a ghost.

CONTRIBUTOR

JESSE THORN is the host and creator of *The Sound of Young America* radio show on Public Radio International, where he has interviewed such guests as Mark Evanier, Weird Al Yankovic, and Judd Apatow. He is also the founder of production organization Maximum Fun (maximumfun.org), as well as the host of *The Grid*, a cultural recommendation program on the Independent Film Channel (IFC). He lives in Los Angeles with his wife, Theresa.